Table of Contents:

We're Sorry

Intro:

Ephesians 2:5-11 In your relationships with one another, have the same mindset as Christ Jesus: Who, being in very nature God, did not consider equality with God something to be used to his own advantage; rather, he made himself nothing by taking the very nature of a servant, being made in human likeness. And being found in appearance as a man, he humbled himself by becoming obedient to death—even death on a cross! Therefore God exalted him to the highest place and gave him the name that is above every name, that at the name of Jesus every knee should bow, in heaven and on earth and under the earth, and every tongue acknowledge that Jesus Christ is Lord, to the glory of God the Father. (NIV)

I was recently at a citywide seminar listening to a star-studded lineup of keynote speakers. A person who has a deep passion for motivating people to succeed in life and "purchase his products" was the benefactor for the event. During the host's forty-five minute sales pitch he prided himself on making shocking comments. While he was speaking he made it very clear he was a Christian. During his talk he said many off color remarks coming across extremely arrogant and crass. One thing he repeatedly said truly offended me and made me want to get this book to print as fast as possible. Multiple times, in the middle of an offensive statement he would say, "If you don't like me that's okay because I'm going to Heaven and you aren't." He made several comments about how God loves him while insinuating that God does not love those who choose not to call themselves Christian. This conference was in a very large arena with over fifteen thousand people in attendance.

I wish I could say he is the only Christian I have ever heard make a comment like this; sadly he is not. I have heard pastors say that very same phrase from pulpits in more than one church. I wish I could ask that man where he got his comment from because I am willing to bet he probably heard it from someone he looks up to in ministry.

Many people see the church as prideful, arrogant, and rude because we often are.

There is no further attribute from Jesus than pride. Jesus was so humble that He left the perfect environment of living with The Father and became a man. He gave up being omnipresent, omniscient, and omnipotent to become a man. He lived a humble life on earth and was tortured by the most horrific form of capital punishment ever known. Dying a criminal's death yet never once sinned. He did that because He is humble and deeply loves all people. He loves us so much that while we were yet sinners He died for us. (Romans 5:8 NIV) He commands us to be the same to others.

As a Pastor for the past twenty-two years I have talked to countless people who have been deeply wounded by the church. In fact I would say the greatest reasons people give for not wanting to follow Jesus is his followers.

Several years ago I read Donald Millers book, "Blue Like Jazz". I was deeply impacted by the story of a confessional booth they set up on the lawn of a very liberal college campus. Students came expecting to confess their sins but were pleasantly shocked as the Christians confessed the sins of the church to them. What an awesome example of humility.

As a Pastor in the Christian Church I am recognizing more and more the many failures I have had in representing Christ. Two years ago our church sent out twelve thousand five hundred, five inch by nine inch "We're Sorry" post cards to our local community. The card was a genuine apology and invitation to the eight-week sermon series we did apologizing for eight major offenses we know we have committed.

I have been writing this book and wrestling with the idea of publishing it ever since. This book has been in the process of being written for the past twenty-four months but in reality it represents my journey in the Christian church for the last three decades since I found Jesus.

More than ever before culture is divided: "The right vs. left": "Liberals vs. Conservatives": "Democrats vs. Republicans": "Church vs. Un-churched": even "Church vs. Church". As Christians we are supposed to represent who Jesus is. It is very easy to blame the other side, claim spiritual high ground, and disregard those who believe differently than we do. As I read scripture Jesus broke down the walls of demarcation and was known as a friend of sinners. Jesus was a friend with the irreligious. He did not separate himself or set himself up as an antagonist or enemy.

I hope and pray this book impacts culture in very meaningful ways: Both Christians as well as non-Christian alike. I hope and pray we will be able to gather round the table of relationship and love and respect each other as human beings who have been given the free will to believe whatever we want to believe. I don't think this is possible without first an act of humility. An apology!

The Christian Church has been wrong in many ways. If you are a Christian I hope and pray you read these words, examine your heart, and ask God to help you know whom you should apologize to and what areas of your life/faith you need to adjust. I must warn you… This will sting a bit.

If you have been hurt by the Christian Church I hope and pray you accept this apology and realize that your pain came from imperfect people not from God. Along with each apology I give explanation and correction of where these behaviors come from in the attempt to help both sides have a deeper understanding of the thinking errors and misbehaviors of the church. I hope and pray this book opens new, honest, respectful, and loving dialogue.

The Christian Church has become known for being hypocritical, money hungry, judgmental, sexually distorted, angry, exclusive, political, and proud. Recognizing our failures is the first step in repentance. We can change if we are willing to humble ourselves and be more like Jesus. Humility often begins with admitting we were wrong and saying "We're Sorry".

Chapter 1:   Hypocritical

"How can you say to your brother, 'Let me take the speck out of your eye,' when all the time there is a plank in your own eye? You hypocrite, first take the plank out of your own eye, and then you will see clearly to remove the speck from your brother's eye." (Jesus Christ) Matthew 7:4 & 5 (NIV)

The greatest tragedy in the history of the Christian church is happening on our watch.   We - The Christian Church – (People who are called Christians) are no longer known for who Jesus truly is. People outside the church first started calling people *Christians* in Antioch, shortly after Christ's resurrection. This label was placed on them because of their character and heart for mankind. The word means "Christlike". When they called them Christians, they were saying they had the heart, compassion, integrity, love, and character of Jesus. Christians of the first century were authentic. They served, accepted, included, loved, helped, and cared for all people; not just religious people, but people who were way outside their comfort zone. They actually went out of their way to find people they could serve. They were like Jesus, so people called them *Christians*.

If you were to ask people outside the church today, to in one word describe the Christian Church, what descriptive word do you think they would use? I hate to admit this but people call us *hypocrites*. The people who call themselves Christians are supposed to represent the most authentic, loving, self-sacrificial, servant to ever walk the planet. Instead of being called authentic "Christ-Like" followers, we are called posers, actor's… hypocrites.

Jesus gave us the task of bringing people back into relationship with the heavenly Father. The Bible calls this the ministry of reconciliation. (2 Corinthians 5:18 NIV) Sadly the number one complaint and greatest obstacle people have in coming to know Jesus are most often His followers. This complaint does not just come from people outside the church. There are many regularly attending churchgoers all over America who echo these same sentiments.

Most people in our culture have enough biblical knowledge to know that God loves people and requires His children to love people as well. If you ask people what the church advocates as the meaning of Christianity you will often hear a lengthy list of rules, regulations, standards, and behaviors that must be adhered to. They are sick of hearing the rules and not seeing the love. They are sick of being what they would describe as, "hated on by haters". They are sick of Christians screaming about standards they despise while at the same time clearly breaking standards the Bible calls sin.

Where did our standards come from?

Jesus was the holiest person to ever live. The Bible says He never sinned; He always did the right thing. He was "righteous". Because of His example and instruction, the Church has stood for the righteousness scripture defines.

The Bible teaches that God created everything and everyone. As "The Creator," He has a plan for His creation. He reveals Himself and His intentions through the life of Jesus and the pages of His letter to mankind – "scripture". Within this letter, we find ways to live and ways not to live. It is not a step-by-step exhaustive map for each individual life, but it does give us excellent guidelines for almost every area of life.

God doesn't micromanage us; He simply gives basic key guidelines. One of my close friends says, "The Bible is more like a compass than a roadmap." I agree. When I take to heart the instruction of scripture and do the things it says, I find myself going in the direction I want to go, and most importantly, ending up in places I want to be. When I behave contrary to scripture, I end up going the wrong direction. The Bible describes living the way God intends for us as "righteousness", and the ways we should not – "sin". Sin is an archery term meaning *to miss the mark.* In the case of scripture, the word *sin* means to miss the mark of God's plan and/or His righteousness.

For instance, if I mismanage my sexuality, choosing to be unfaithful to my wife. The Bible calls this sin *"adultery"*. This may bring some pleasure for a short time, but the result is a wife who has a broken heart and no longer trusts me. This lack of trust will affect every part of our relationship and most likely destroy our marriage. Adultery is missing the mark of God. It not only separates me from God, it ruins God's plan for

Tina and I to have a wonderfully happy, and amazing relationship with each other. This one sin has drastic affects on the entire family.

Sexual sin seems to be a favorite for the church to highlight, so let's use another example. If I mismanage my eating habits, choosing to eat the wrong foods, constantly stuffing myself, the Bible calls this sin *"gluttony"*. The result of gluttony is unwanted weight gain and a myriad of physical complications. This would be missing God's mark for the health of my body. Thousands of people are prisoners in their own skin. Like all sin, there are spiritual as well as natural consequences. Because God loves us, He is concerned with both.

It seems in the North American church today there are acceptable and unacceptable sins. Gluttony seems to be a sin the Church not only participates in, we often joke about, laughing it off as if it is a "misdemeanor" sin. I could go on and on with examples of sins the Church readily admits and laughs about. The truth is, we Christians struggle with all kinds of sin. The reason for using these examples is to illustrate the Bible clearly defines missing God's mark. In fact, the Bible says everyone has missed the mark of God's holiness.

God has written a moral code and placed it in the hearts of mankind. In addition He has defined what it means to miss His mark, "sin". It seems the Christian Church vehemently condemns some sins, while actively participating in others. The reason we need to apologize is not because we believe in God, the Bible, or the fact we acknowledge sin is wrong. The reason we must apologize is because we have condemned people for sins we deem as "intolerable," while we ourselves, participate in sins we deem acceptable. Not only have we arrogantly put ourselves in the place of judge, we have also become the jury, convicting ourselves in scandal after scandal, doing the very things we condemn. We have been hypocritical, all the while portraying a holier-than-thou, self-righteous, condemning attitude. It's time "we" the Church own up to our failure.

We have earned the "Hypocrite" label

It's important to recognize all people have hypocrisy in them at some level. For instance, earlier I spoke of gluttony. I personally have the value of eating right, staying in shape, and looking and feeling my best. With that said, we just went through the Thanksgiving and Christmas holidays. You can see where I am going with this. During these past few months, I overate almost everyday. Not only did I overeat at home, I really enjoyed all the snacks people brought into the office. I claim to have the virtue of eating right and staying in shape. Yet, in these past two months, I have gone backwards on that commitment. I think I gained ten pounds. How about you? Are there values and virtues you aspire to, yet don't always actively live out? I wish I could say food was the only failure I have. If I did, I would not only be a hypocrite, I would be a liar as well.

We all aspire to hold many virtuous values that aren't always lived up to in our daily lives. When it comes to Biblical and spiritual virtues, followers of Christ are expected to uphold them all. As Romans 7 clearly teaches. The truth is, there are things we want to do that we don't do, and things we don't want to do that we do do. Yes, do-do. That's exactly what it is. Sadly, many people who call themselves Christians are blatantly and willfully disobedient to Christ, living the way they want to live regardless of the loving direction of God. The people who are close to us know this. In fact, people who don't know us, see them as well. We must call it what it is. It is hypocrisy.

I wish it were untrue, but I'm afraid we have earned the hypocrite label. Millions of people have experienced hatred instead of *love*; anger instead of *joy*; violence and rage instead of *peace*; intolerance instead of *patience*; wrath instead of *kindness*; deceit instead of *goodness*; brutality instead of *gentleness*; abandonment instead of *faithfulness*; and arrogance instead of *self-control*. The very things that are supposed to grow out of a Christ-follower's life – "Fruit of The Spirit (Galatians 5:22-23), are the antithesis of what society feels they are experiencing. In our pride, we have the audacity to tell others what is wrong with them while we ourselves have so much wrong with us.

Why are so many people so ticked off?

In addition to sending out 12,000 "We're Sorry" post cards to our community we also did a major press release letting the media know of our public apology. One of the major city newspapers interviewed me and did a great story: "Local Christian Pastor Says He's Sorry." I sent the columnist the postcard to help explain what we were doing. The card was on her desk less than an hour, when a co-worker walked by and asked what it was. She started to explain, but before she could get through her thoughts, he emphatically interrupted, "You tell that pastor, I don't accept his apology!" She didn't say anything; she just looked at him wondering what was triggering such anger. He immediately launched into his bad experiences with the Christian Church. Just a piece of paper on a desk, an apology nonetheless, caused a grown man to re-live his pain and become visibly and audibly irate. Jesus gave us very clear warning about this.

Matthew 7:1-6 "Do not judge others, and you will not be judged. For you will be treated as you treat others. The standard you use in judging is the standard by which you will be judged. "And why worry about a speck in your friend's eye when you have a log in your own? How can you think of saying to your friend, 'Let me help you get rid of that speck in your eye,' when you can't see past the log in your own eye? Hypocrite! First get rid of the log in your own eye; then you will see well enough to deal with the speck in your friend's eye. Don't waste what is holy on people who are unholy. Don't throw your pearls to pigs! They will trample the pearls, then turn and attack you." (NLT)

Jesus began this passage by instructing us not to judge people. Judgment is another major source of contention with people outside the church. After being instructed not to judge, Jesus gives us a very practical reason not to. He says, "You will be treated the way you treat others." Our newspaper columnist's co-worker was obviously mistreated in a local church. His awful experience caused so much pain he no longer wants anything to do with Christians or the church. He is hurt and angry and wants everyone to know it. People will treat you the way you treat them. It didn't matter that I had never met him nor was his bad experience in our church. Christians not only represent Jesus, we represent His Church. Somewhere on this man's journey, the Church significantly hurt him.

We wonder why the homosexual community or the pro-choice community is so angry with the Church? I think it is obvious! Please allow me to jump on my soapbox and be very bold here. If you're one of those "Christians" holding up the "God hates fags" sign, could you please stop spreading that horrible lie? If you are one of those "Christians" who bomb the abortion clinics would you please stop hating people with the "Love of Jesus"? Love and hate are two things that don't go together. God does not hate people. God loves all people so much that He gave His one and only Son, so they could have a vibrant, personal relationship with Him.

The problem isn't just the hateful people shouting at the top of their lungs. It's the quiet Sunday schoolteacher who ran off with the local church pastor, or the friend who judged them and said "turn or burn", or the Christian gossip around the lunch table at work.

In Mathew 7 Jesus continued with an amazing visual example. Imagine someone trying to point out a speck of dust in your eye, while they have a plank jammed in theirs. *"The only thing a person has to gain when casting spiritual judgment on another is hypocrisy."* When one person points out the faults in another person's life while at the same time struggle with faults of their own, "sometimes the very same issues", the Bible calls this "plank eye". Many people point out a speck in someone else's eye when all along there is a giant plank in their own. Since we all struggle with sin Jesus tells us not to judge others. If we do it will tick them off and expose us as hypocritical.

If we proclaim the Bible as our authority for life, people naturally assume we ascribe to the whole book. Yet the Church is well known for gossip, slander, anger, hatred, envy, greed, pride, gluttony, fits of rage, lust, and many more sins the Bible clearly commands us to abstain from. We have bumper stickers that say, "Christians aren't perfect, just forgiven." We say things like, "We all struggle with sin." Yes, those are both true, but we laugh about blatant sins while treating people like trash over sins we classify as "more" heinous. Can we really blame them for being enraged? We not only have a plank in our eye, we have a huge stack of lumber on the side of our life we constantly must divert their attention from. Many act as if shouting about others issues while threatening eternal damnation wins the argument.

Smokescreen Christianity

Have you ever been in a tense discussion with someone, where you are making a very compelling argument, and then all of the sudden find the subject suddenly and radically changed? If so, you have experienced a smokescreen. When we have something we don't want others to see we often create a smokescreen to divert attention from whatever it is we are hiding.

Often, when Christians are confronted with sin they feel attacked so they lash out. In addition when people ask intelligent questions highlighting their objections to faith, many Christian's are not prepared to answer. Their unpreparedness comes across as frustration or anger. When either of these scenarios comes about, we often feel as though we are losing, so we react by bringing up something else to give us better leverage. The barrage of new issues turns into a whirlwind, diverting attention from the issue at hand. If someone asks an intelligent question that is contrary to our beliefs, we bring up the issue of eternal damnation. If someone points out something wrong with us, or the Church, we bring up the sins of others-using words like *abomination* and *debauchery*. We may feel as though we are making headway in our position, but in reality, most people think of us as arrogant, unprepared, ignorant, hateful, hypocrites.

All people struggle with sin, including Christians. Most Christians feel great pressure knowing they are supposed to be Christ like. Because of these pressures, we often try to portray ourselves as if we have no sin in our lives or as if the sins we do commit are minor. I have often wondered why so many Christian's body language, tone, volume, and looks become so irate when talking about sexual sin, murder, or abortion? It's a smokescreen. Yelling loudly about sins that make us personally uncomfortable is a diversion from our own personal shortcomings.

The Church compares itself to the rest of society and acts as if God is grading on a curve. We point the finger at sexual sin, especially homosexuality, lesbianism, and adultery. We point the finger at murderers and thieves. Then threaten hell and eternal damnation for anyone who doesn't conform to our beliefs. Our attitude comes across as condescending and full of hate. Jesus was known as a friend of sinners, we are known as hypocritical haters.

Sadly, many Christians don't hold to the standards they so boldly condemn. Not a year goes by we don't see news headlines highlighting a nationally known pastor, evangelist, or priest caught in yet another scandal. It's not just the high profile cases that are killing us. Sunday school teachers, choir members, and youth leaders are running off with people other than their spouse in the Church. People are gossiping, slandering, and even violently hurting people inside the Church. The divorce rate is just as high in the Church as it is outside.

Jesus predicted what would happen if we take such a posture. If we go around spouting off scripture, acting better and holier-than-thou, it ticks people off. That is why there is so much animosity and friction towards the church. Jesus died so all people can be forgiven. He said He would wash away every log and speck. Jesus washes away every sin and the Holy Spirit convicts. Our part in the equation is reconciliation.

Many Christians feel like they are letting Jesus down if they don't tell people how bad their sins are and how much they disapprove. We must realize we are not condoning a person's sin if we don't condemn it. We are merely being kind, compassionate, and loving. It is not that sin isn't sin. Sin is missing the standard of God. *"The standard of God!"* It is not *our* standard to uphold or defend. Smokescreen religion may win an argument, but the casualty of lost credibility and true friendships is far too high a price to pay.

The problem isn't the Bible, nor is it Jesus. The problem is us!

God gave His one and only Son, so all people can be restored in relationship with Him. This is the most gracious act of mercy I can imagine. Jesus gave His life to pay our penalty of death. This is the most amazing act of love ever. People aren't rejecting God or His Son Jesus. People are rejecting Christians because of our attitude and approach. The Church has used the threat of Hell and eternal damnation as its trump card to win every argument. When we are unable to answer a question or refute an intelligent argument we threaten them with the worst threat of all: If you don't conform to what we believe, you will go to Hell. In fact, by our tone and posture, they feel as if we are glad they might go there. This is not only rude; it is arrogant, manipulative, and hateful.

We feel threatened by anyone who doesn't believe everything we believe. At the sight of even the slightest threat we rear back and let them have it. The shame of it is, many people who question faith are genuinely asking heartfelt questions for which they desperately want answers.

I was a Youth Pastor for fifteen years. Over those years I had many kids tell me stories of how they were unable to question faith to their parents. Questions and objections were considered blasphemous. How sad that so many Christians act as if God is not big enough or intelligent enough to handle our questions. Many adults who grew up attending church no longer attend or want anything to do with God because they think God is like their parents or people at the church they left.

We have not only been mean, we have been incredibly arrogant and self-righteous. People are God's creation. God loves and Jesus died for all people, and we are repelling them. This is a huge offense! Not just to people, but to God.

James 2:8-13 "Yes indeed, it is good when you obey the royal law as found in the Scriptures: 'Love your neighbor as yourself.' But if you favor some people over others, you are committing a sin. You are guilty of breaking the law. For the person who keeps all of the laws except one is as guilty as a person who has broken all of God's laws. For the same God who said, 'You must not commit adultery,' also said, 'You must not murder.' So if you murder someone but do not commit

adultery, you have still broken the law. So whatever you
say or whatever you do, remember that you will be judged by
the law that sets you free. There will be no mercy for those who
have not shown mercy to others. But if you have been merciful,
God will be merciful when he judges you." (NLT)

Loving our neighbor as we love ourselves is keeping the royal law found in scripture. Not loving our neighbor as we love ourselves is breaking the royal law of scripture. Breaking one law in scripture has the same consequence in the spiritual realm as breaking all the laws in scripture. Favoring one person over another is breaking the law of God. Treating some people better than we treat others is sinful. The scariest part about what James is teaching is, if we treat people who agree with our theology better than we treat people who don't, we are committing sin.

Loving our neighbors as we love ourselves is the perfect place to start. The key question is: When I am with people who don't have the same beliefs I have, do I treat them with the same respect and kindness with which I want them to treat me? Likewise, when I share my faith with people, do I treat them the way I would want them to treat me?

Lets say someone comes to share their faith with us. Do we want that person to come calling us names and threatening to kill us if we don't convert? Absolutely not! I don't know of any Christians threatening physical violence to people in today's world. It is important to note that in times past, professing Christians did kill non-converts and that was beyond wrong. I am very sorry that is part of Christian history, and I am extremely sorry to anyone whose family was impacted by those heinous crimes. Christians today don't threaten people with physical harm, we threaten much worse: eternal damnation in Hell. We call this love?

Someone recently gave me a newspaper article that was written by a proclaiming Christian. She said, "Seldom does a day go by when some **snob** in the **liberal** blogosphere isn't bashing Christianity." I might be wrong here, but… isn't calling someone a *snob,* bashing? Is this treating others how we want to be treated? We become so easily offended by the way people talk about us; yet we do the same thing or worse to them.

The very fact we are un-loving makes us a lawbreaker. We are viewed as hypocrites, because we deserve it. As Christians who study God's Word, we should know better. Just because we may not have murdered, does not mean we are innocent. This is why Jesus was so strong about us forgiving others. Jesus forgave us of every wrong we have ever done. We don't even have the freedom to be rude to people who openly bash us. We must remember Jesus allowed people to strip, beat, put a crown of thorns on His head, spit on Him, and nail Him to a cross. After they did all that, He asked the Father to forgive them. We have a hard time being cordial to people simply using words.

The "Hypocrite" perception (can and must) change.

In North America today, there is a tremendous amount of

friction between Christians and non-Christians. Both sides demand "their rights". Both sides are entrenched in their philosophies and morals, and both sides hurl grenades from their bunkers as often as possible. Problems are not being solved, nor is the love of Christ being shown. As followers of Christ, we are not supposed to be throwing grenades. We are supposed to be engaged in peace talks. The word "reconcile" means to bring together, reunite, resolve, settle, or patch up.

Many Christians have segregated themselves, their children, and their church organizations from the outside world. They live in a subculture of protection and isolation. Many Christians have interpreted 2 Corinthians 6:17, where we are instructed to come out from among them and be *separate*, as come out and be *separated.* In this passage, we are instructed to be different, peculiar, not the same. We are to be different when it comes to sinful behavior not separated or divided. If we are supposed to be separated, Jesus would not have been known as a friend of sinners, nor would He have instructed us to go to the entire world.

The Bible says we are the ambassadors of God. Meaning we represent Him to the world. Jesus has forgiven their sin and washed it away making them whiter than snow. All they need to do is ask for forgiveness and turn their lives over to Him. Sadly we are often the ones holding them back.

2 Corinthians 5:17-19 "Therefore, if anyone is in Christ, the new creation has come: The old has gone, the new is here! All this is from God, who reconciled us to himself through Christ and gave us the ministry of reconciliation: that God was

reconciling the world to himself in Christ, not counting
people's sins against them. And he has committed to us the
message of reconciliation." (NIV)

Is there animosity, anger, and friction? Yes! But, where there is friction, there is great traction. This is something that can be fixed. The solution is simple but it may be one of the most difficult things we ever do.

Admitting we have been hypocritical is a great place to start. We are not perfect. We have blown it in many ways. Humbly admitting we have not always represented the love, character, or actions of Christ can start to rebuild relationships. Forgiving people and not counting their sins against them is crucial. We must stop pointing out what is wrong with everyone else. And we can't stop there. If we are going to be known for the character of Christ, we must dig deeper.

Lets talk about sin for a second. There are two types of sin. The first is *willful disobedience*. Willful disobedience understands what scripture deems as sin, but then says I don't care what scripture instructs I am going to do it anyways. For example, if we know how God wants us to manage our sexuality, yet choose to act contrary to His direction, we are being willfully disobedient. Likewise, if we know God wants us to forgive all people, but choose to harbor bitterness, resentment, and hatred; we are being willfully disobedient.

The second kind of sin is described in the book of Romans as *struggling with sin.* It is a literal struggle. There are things we know are wrong, and do not want to do. Yet we struggle with the temptation of doing them. We hate ourselves for doing them and try our hardest to abstain while constantly pleading with God to help us stop.

If we are going to be known for the character of Christ, we are going to have to overcome sin. If we don't want to be known for hypocrisy, we have to stop being hypocrites. First, we have to stop willfully sinning. If we call ourselves Christians/Christ-like, then we must be like Jesus. If we are doing things we know are wrong, choosing our pleasure over following Christ, and willfully disobeying, we need to either stop doing those things or stop saying we are following Jesus.

I like to think of being a Christ-follower like hiking with Jesus. The way Jesus knows we are following Him is when He looks back we are there. We can't say we are following Jesus while we choose to mismanage our sexuality, money, greed, appetite, forgiveness, anger, or any other area where we choose to willfully disobey.

Jesus is nowhere near any of these things. How can we claim to follow him yet willfully walk away from him? I am not making a judgment on whether a person will or will not go to Heaven. That is not my place. However, I am saying to willfully disobey and call yourself a Christian is hypocritical. This should cause personal introspection and some healthy fear of the Lord. Jesus is not a hypocrite. As I read scripture, I don't think it is possible to be a Christian/Christ-like and a hypocrite at the same time. Jesus is the genuine article. He is authentic. To follow Him, we must strive to be like Him.

If you are struggling with sin areas that you absolutely

don't want to do, it is time to pursue health. If you truly want to stop, it is time to bring it into the light and walk with some brothers or sisters you can trust.

I will never forget one Monday morning as I was meeting with my accountability partner, I felt impressed by God to tell him about a certain person, who was not my wife, that I was struggling with in my thought life. Towards the end of our prayer time it seemed we had nothing more to pray about so we just sat in silence. My heart was racing as God kept urging me to confess. We sat there in silence for what seemed to be an eternity. I was desperately hoping he would say amen and have to rush off to an appointment, but we just sat. Finally, I mustered up the courage to speak. I had been struggling with these thoughts for a couple of months. Week after week, we met for prayer and accountability, and I had said nothing. As soon as I did, I felt the power of that temptation begin to break. My accountability partner opened the Bible and read 1 John 1. "To walk in the light as He is in the light and if we do we will have fellowship with one another." I prayed for forgiveness for my thoughts and he prayed for God to help me overcome them.

From that day on, each week, two standard questions we asked were, "How is your thought life?" and "How is your marriage?" That was over eighteen years ago, and to this day, I still meet every week with an accountability partner. We answer those questions, as well as others. Then, we pray for each other because we are not above temptation nor are we immune to falling into sin. Over the years, there have been many more weeks where I have had to confess and ask for prayer. We need help from people I can trust. This is a Biblical principal and it works.

In conjunction with living in authentic friendships, you may need to get some help. Professional help if needed. There are people who are trained in helping us unpack why we do the things we do. If you need counseling, get some! If you need to talk with a pastor, do it! If you need prayer, ask someone you can trust! Whatever you need to do, do it. For the sake of the name we represent, Jesus Christ, we should be willing to do whatever it takes to represent Him the very best we can. I have heard people say they can't afford it. We can't afford NOT to. It is far cheaper to spend time and money now, than suffer the consequences both in this life and in the life to come.

We are so sorry for being hypocrites

I wish I could say I have not ever been hypocritical, but I have. Because of this, I have not represented Jesus the way He deserves to be represented; I am part of the reason He is known in our culture for hypocrisy. I am so sorry. If I have hurt you, I hope you can forgive me. If you have been hurt by the Christian Church? I hope you can forgive us.

Practical steps

Take time to pray and ask God some serious questions. As you do, write down what He impresses on your heart and mind.

Then, if you have the guts??? Take action! You may need to make some heartfelt apologies. You may need to get some help with your struggles. Write down your answers to these prayers and give yourself a timeline of action.

1. Lord, are there areas in my life where I willfully disobey you?

2. Lord, these are the sins I struggle with. Please forgive me and help me stop doing them.

3. Lord, who is a person I could trust to be in an accountability relationship with? Please lead me to them? (Best to have guys with guys and girls with girls)

4. Lord, are there people in my life whom I have judged, treated poorly, or whom I have not represented you well with? Do I need to apologize?

5. Lord, you know I feel deeply hurt by people in your church. Please help me forgive them.

6. Lord, please help me recognize the pain I contributed as well.

   a. What pain have I caused?

Chapter 2:   Money Hungry

*2 Corinthians 9:6-11 "Remember this: Whoever sows sparingly will also reap sparingly, and whoever sows generously will also reap generously. Each man should give what he has decided in his heart to give, not reluctantly or under compulsion, for God loves a cheerful giver. And God is able to make all grace abound to you, so that in all things at all times, having all that you need, you will abound in every good work. As it is written: 'He has scattered abroad his gifts to the poor; his righteousness endures forever.' Now he who supplies seed to the sower and bread for food will also supply and increase your store of seed and will enlarge the harvest of your righteousness. **You will be made rich in every way so that you can be generous on every occasion**, and through us your generosity will result in thanksgiving to God." (NIV) (Bold added)*

Saying we're money hungry is another way of saying greedy. Nobody, myself included, likes to be thought of as greedy. The question is: *Are we?* Before you answer, please give careful thought to this question. What do you think people who are outside the Church (not Christ-Followers) would say if we were to ask, "What do you think the Church wants from you?" If your answer is money, you have responded with the same answer I have received from dozens of audiences all over

North America. It seems universally true, the Church is known for wanting money. The tragedy isn't that people think we want their money. The tragedy is they think we want *anything* period.

Jesus came to seek and to save those who are lost. He said He came to serve, not to be served. He said He came to lay down His life as a ransom for many. Jesus not only laid claim to these things, He lived them out while teaching His disciples/followers to do the same. The most loving, caring, and sacrificial person to ever live has become known for... "I want your money"! How has this happened? How have the followers of Christ, the people who represent Him, His ambassadors, how have we allowed the name of Jesus to become known for taking?

The temptation is to personally let ourselves off the hook, pointing to the countless financial scandals we see on the news year after year. It seems not a year goes by we don't hear of a Christian leader misappropriating or embezzling finances. It would be easier if we could blame these scandals on one denomination, but they have occurred in most, if not all. Some of these scandals are blatant, rip-off scams while others are well-meaning people who misappropriate funds.

Trust is all we have

As a young college student studying to become a pastor, I often watched an unnamed televangelist, because of his extreme cheese-mo. I ashamedly admit I tuned in only to judge and mock. One day while channel surfing, his face came across the screen of a 20/20 special. Immediately, I hushed the room to give the broadcast our full attention. In a fundraising effort, the televangelist regularly asked people to trace their handprint on a piece of paper, promising if they would send their traced print, along with a sizeable check, he would place his hand on their hand and pray for them by name. Thousands of people sent in large checks, along with their carefully traced handprints of desperate prayer requests. Broken relationships, cancer, bankruptcy, - serious heartfelt, gut wrenching needs. As it turned out, he never opened even one of them. In fact, not even an intern in the ministry opened the envelopes. Not a single person in this ministry was fulfilling the promise to pray for the thousands of people who generously gave. In stead the letters went directly to the bank where tellers left the letters of plight undisturbed, while depositing the checks that accompanied them. 20/20 discovered the envelopes in the bank's dumpster in the back alley.

You may have seen this scandal, too? If not, you probably have many others in mind. I wish I could say this problem was relegated to TV personalities alone. But it isn't that simple. I just recently saw in our local newspaper another headline and full front-page story of a local pastor embezzling funds from his congregation. I'm sure you have seen your fair share of these as well. It isn't just church leaders either. How many times have we heard of professing Christians ripping people off in business?

The truth is, money is one of the greatest temptations of all.

In Bible college, our professors told many stories of misappropriation of funds; many of which were perpetrated from sheer ignorance, others blatant theft. Each story came with a stern warning. "As ministers we must understand and adhere to the strictest of accounting standards as well as personally know what our organization is doing with money."

In ministry, all you have is trust. When you lose trust, you lose everything. Money is one of the most scrutinized issues we deal with. It takes years and years to build trust and only seconds to lose it.

The first church I worked at was a very large church with excellent accounting practices. It was a great place to learn how to be a pastor and manage money. As the Junior High Pastor, I often took pizzas to local junior high schools during their lunch period. It was a great way to build relationships with kids while totally making their day. My staff members and I would bring dozens of pizzas each time we went. The first time we went out to "feed the hungry" our business manager stopped me in the hall to clarify the financial process in which we were providing the grub. He said, "I heard you took pizzas to the kids at lunch. That's really cool. How did you pay for the food?" I replied, "I paid out of my own pocket and the kids reimbursed me." He asked if I had their money with me and kept the receipt. I said yes with a questioning look on my face. He then said, "In this case, you will need to give me the receipt." The two of us counted the money, put it in an envelope, and both signed for the amount.

In the feeding of the masses that followed, as well as all

other money interactions a check request for reimbursement was run through the accounting office and youth budget accounts. Myself and a volunteer staff member would count monies received, seal it in an envelope, sign the envelope, and turn it in with the receipt." He explained how this would create a paper trail protecting the church and me from possible accusations.

Six months later, with twice as many kids coming to our pizza days, one of the boys jokingly said, "Dude, you are making so much money off of us." I quickly let him know that we were not making money by feeding junior high kids; in fact, we always lost money doing this. I let him know we have a very clear record of every penny spent at the church. He said, "Dude, relax I was just kidding." I explained to him why we never joke about money at the church. Money is far too important of an issue to make light of. I can't imagine what could have happened if that kid went home telling his parents we were profiting from junior high students at lunch. That never happened, but if it had and we had not keep excellent records, I would be in big trouble and the Church could have lost trust in our community.

In ministry or business, we must be acutely aware that money is a huge temptation. Money is a very serious issue we must always account for. For this reason we must constantly prove ourselves trustworthy by managing all our resources with the utmost integrity.

The Church has become known for being money hungry because of mismanagement within our organizations as well as mismanagement of its individual members. Whenever a church, church leader, or even a professing Christ Follower mismanages their business dealings or personal resources it puts a stain on the name of Christ. There is a reality we must come to terms with; we have lost the trust in our communities.

As we walk through this topic, I want to address the Church as an organizationally as well as individuals.

Is money evil?

The Church has differing viewpoints when it comes to money. On one end of the spectrum, some churches preach a prosperity gospel, claiming all Christians should be blessed with wealth and prosperity because they follow the God who owns everything. On the opposite swing of that pendulum, some churches preach money is evil and nothing good comes from money; therefore, the ideal Christian lifestyle is to live a monastic life proving your true devotion and utter dependence on God.

1st Timothy 6:10 "For the love of money is a root of all kinds of evil. Some people, eager for money, have wandered from the faith and pierced themselves with many grief's."
(NIV)

While growing up, I heard many people misquote this verse saying, "The love of money is the root of *"all"* evil". Saying money is the root of "all evil" implies money in and of itself is evil and should be avoided by all. Money is one of the strongest temptations in life and many evil things have been done in the pursuit of money. Ironically, you can't do much good without it. Money is not the root of evil; the devil is the root of evil. Money can be used for evil or good, but by itself, it is just money.

Personally, I pray God helps me provide for my family, and help others all the time. The way we provide food, shelter, clothing, and all other needs of our family is by earning money. In fact, we spend at least one-third of our waking hours earning money. Whether you are a business, church, non-profit agency, family, or single person, you need money to survive. When you have it, money is a needed blessing. The Bible says all good and perfect gifts come from The Lord. Money isn't perfect, but it certainly meets many needs. Money in and of itself is not evil, just like computers, the Internet, automobiles, and telephones in and of themselves are not evil. All of these things can be used for evil or good. How we manage money is the determining factor for evil or good.

$ Whose is it?

King David was the second king of the Israelite nation. Like most of us, David had many struggles with sin in his life. Yet with all his faults he is known in scripture as a man after God's own heart. At the end of his life, David donates a huge portion of his wealth to the building project of the temple of The Lord. All the Israelites join him in being generous to this cause. When he and the people make this enormous donation here is what he says:

*1 Chronicles 29:10-14 "David praised the LORD in the presence of the whole assembly, saying, 'Praise be to you, O LORD, God of our father Israel, from everlasting to everlasting. Yours, O LORD, is the greatness and the power and the glory and the majesty and the splendor, for everything in heaven and earth is yours. Yours, O LORD, is the kingdom; you are exalted as head over all. Wealth and honor come from you; you are the ruler of all things. In your hands are strength and power to exalt and give strength to all. Now, our God, we give you thanks, and praise your glorious name. **But who am I, and who are my people, that we should be able to give as generously as this? Everything comes from you, and we have given you only what comes from your hand.** '" (NIV)(Bold added)*

In the course of making large donations, many people bring attention to themselves, pointing out their generous. We seem to enjoy having buildings named in our honor and plaques placed on items we donate. We pretend this is a way to say thank you and encourage others to give, but deep down, we like to have notoriety for being such generous people. After David's generous donations he says, "Everything I have comes from God, I did not deserve it nor do I take the credit for earning it. Everything I have is from God." Standing in awe of the blessed life he has lived, he seems almost dumbfounded as he asks, "Who am I?" David was not from wealth or royalty; he was just a small shepherd boy when God gave him the courage to face Goliath. Resisting the temptation to take credit for all his achievements and bolster his nobility, he is truly humble asking, "Who am I."

All blessings come from God, including money. Some Christians have buckets of money while others are barely able to feed their families. From a global perspective the amount of money people have is absolutely in no way a reflection of how fervently they follow God.

In North America we are incredibly blessed. Some people recognize this blessing comes from God and others do not. Whose is it? From a biblical perspective there is only one answer. God allows us free will in every area of our lives, including money. Whose is it, is an essential question to the condition of our hearts.

$ Tricky $

Money is a needed blessing that can become a destructive obsession. Having the opportunity to earn money and amass possessions is an amazing blessing. Living in this country affords us many opportunities that most people around the globe have no idea exist. These amazing opportunities for wealth can be very tricky. Look carefully how Jesus progresses through this teaching.

Matthew 6:19-24 "Do not store up for yourselves treasures
on earth, where moth and rust destroy, and where thieves
break in and steal. But store up for yourselves treasures in
heaven, where moth and rust do not destroy, and where thieves
do not break in and steal. For where your treasure is, there
your heart will be also. The eye is the lamp of the body. If your
eyes are good, your whole body will be full of light. But if your
eyes are bad, your whole body will be full of darkness. If then
the light within you is darkness, how great is that darkness! No
one can serve two masters. Either you will hate the one and
love the other, or you will be devoted to the one and despise the
other. ***You cannot serve both God and money.****" (NIV)(Bold*
added)

To those of us whom attend church, Jesus ends this teaching with a very familiar quote, "You cannot serve both God and money." I love how Jesus builds up to this statement. Our stuff on earth is going to stay on earth. All the things we so feverishly work for is destined for the scrap heap, so, be careful not to build up all your treasure here.

Jesus points to a place you can build up treasure where it will last forever. Heaven has a place with your name on it and there are things you can do in this life that will build up treasure there. Your treasure in Heaven will never go away, so which is a better place to invest? The obvious answer is to build up treasure where it will last.

We see throughout scripture the good we do for others we are also doing for Jesus. If we help someone in prison, it is helping Him. If we feed the poor, it is feeding Him. Even giving someone a cup of cool water in His name will not be overlooked. If you have children, you understand how grateful you are when people help your kids. God made every person on the planet. When we serve, help, or give to any of them, we are helping His kids. He does not overlook even the smallest gift.

Amidst so much blessing in our country, one of the strongest temptations we face is to put all of our work into building what we can see, touch, and possess "now" rather than investing for eternity.

Jesus began this teaching with investments; next he talks about our eyes. Do you remember the song, "Be careful little eyes what you see. Be careful little eyes what you see. For the Father up above is looking down in love, so be careful little eyes what you see." It had other verses, too, but that one came straight out of what Jesus is saying here. The things we see motivate us in all kinds of ways.

Throughout my adult life, I have chosen to submit myself to one or two other guys I can trust as accountability partners. One day, we were meeting for lunch at Applebee's and the subject of pornography came up. Both of my friends started looking at pornography when they were in elementary school. By the time they were in high school, it was a full-throttle addiction. For one of them, pornography ruined his first marriage. For the other, he and his wife went through extensive counseling and received help. They had both overcome the addiction through tons of prayer, counseling, twelve-step groups, and accountability. I was uncharacteristically quiet as they talked.

They noticed my silence and started razing me for not being engaged in the conversation. I had to explain that there were two reasons for my unusual silence. First, I made it very clear I was not putting myself above them or claiming to be without sin, but pornography has never been an issue in my life. My family was very open about sexual issues when I was growing up, and my mom started talking to me about porn when I was in the sixth grade. She had convinced me porn was demonic; if I messed with it, I was inviting the devil into my life. Those statements I believe are absolutely true and that was enough to keep me from that trap.

I continued with the main reason I was not in the conversation. I said, "Porn has never been a problem for me, but that (pointing out the window at a red Dodge Viper across the street) is a major problem." They laughed and blew it off like I was joking. I continued, "This is a huge issue for me. I love shiny, fast stuff! As we have been sitting here, I have been lusting after that car. I am trying to figure out how I can finance it, sell a kid for it, or do whatever it takes to have that in my garage."

That is just one example of the many things I want and can't afford. In reality, for me to own a car like that I would have to live in it. We can very easily fall in love/lust with stuff. When we do, we start living for and serving it. Be careful little eyes what you see!

America, and much of the rest of the world, relies on our

consumerism for their existence. We are the ultimate consumers. We don't mind being called consumers, but what if we used another word? Greed! Some have misinterpreted the quote from Jesus in Matthew 6:24 as "you cannot have money and serve God." Jesus is not saying it is wrong to have money. You can have money and serve God, but you can't "serve money" and serve God. How do we know if we are serving money or not? This is not the only barometer for measuring our service, but one major indicator might be our debt.

We recently went through the greatest recession since the great depression because we live way beyond our means. Americans finance everything, including our homes. Financing a home is not always a bad idea, because we either pay rent or a mortgage. But, many Americans have viewed their home as a giant piggybank to crack open, in the form of home equity loans, to pay for all the things we lust for.

We finance our cars. Cars are a necessary item in our society. We need them to get to work, take our kids to school, and go everywhere else. It seems we have three choices: pay cash for a beater and put money into maintenance, pay huge payments on a new car with a warranty, or save for a good car while driving a beater. Either way, cars are nothing but a money pit where we lose money. But, we don't stop at homes and cars; we finance boats, RV's, and vacation property. We even put vacations on our credit cards, paying eighteen percent or higher interest for years after our enjoyment. We finance our stereo systems, flat screen TV's, and furniture. We finance our Adidas, Nike's, and Levis. Many people are financing their groceries and gas to drive to work. How crazy will it become before we learn? We are paying interest on something we pooped out over a year ago. When the debt becomes too much, we reach into our giant piggybank and refinance it for thirty more years. Paying for a pair of shoes or a TV for thirty years is just plain crazy.

America is stuck right now! Not because the government encouraged home loans for anyone with a pulse and social security number. That didn't help, but no one has been holding a gun to anyone's head making them borrow money. We are stuck because of our greed. We owe, we owe, it's off to work we go. If you know what it feels like to have way more month at the end of your money, you understand what the Bible says about becoming a servant/slave to the lender. Many Christians are literally serving *"money and stuff"*. It's not fair to blame our problems on the government, the televangelist, the economy, or anything else. ***We fell in love with it, we had to have it, we signed our name for it, and now we have to serve it.*** Am I saying that debt is sinful? No, I am not. In fact, there are countless scriptures instructing those who lend money to do it ethically. God would not instruct lenders how to lend and then tell everyone not to have a loan. But, He did say that we are servant to the lender because he fully expects us to honor our word and pay it back. I think we might have it backwards. ***Money should serve us, not us serve money.*** Is it possible that we have been duped?

$ TRAP $

I realize it is incredibly insulting to be called greedy. So I want to be clear that I am not trying to set up parameters to personally judge anyone. With that said I do hope you are strong enough to consider a very serious internal inventory that answers this question honestly to yourself and to God. Most people don't set goals to be greedy; we simply get trapped. Check out the wisdom of Christ.

Luke 12:13-21 "Someone in the crowd said to him, 'Teacher, tell my brother to divide the inheritance with me.' Jesus replied, 'Man, who appointed me a judge or an arbiter between you?' Then he said to them, 'Watch out! Be on your guard against all kinds of greed; a man's life does not consist in an abundance of his possessions.' And he told them this parable: 'The ground of a certain rich man produced a good crop. He thought to himself, 'What shall I do? I have no place to store my crops.' Then he said, 'This is what I'll do. I will tear down my barns and build bigger ones, and there I will store all my grain and my goods. And I'll say to myself, 'You have plenty of good things laid up for many years. Take life easy; eat, drink and be merry.' But God said to him, 'You fool! This very night your life will be demanded from you. Then who will get what you have prepared for yourself?' This is how it will be with whoever stores up things for themselves but is not rich toward God." (NIV)

If you have ever seen siblings fight over an inheritance, you understand why Jesus so brilliantly sidestepped this guy's issue. To help him get a grasp on material possessions, Jesus tells him a little story. This wealthy businessman has a banner year. The barns that had always been ample for his provision now seemed too small to contain such an overwhelming harvest. Instead of doing something to help others or serve God, he chooses to set himself up and live the good life. No sooner are his new barns finished, he dies. Jesus asks, "Now who is going to fight over his stuff?"

In light of how amazingly blessed we are in North America; this is a story we should take to heart. It blows me away to hear so many Christians refer to themselves as poor. There are just over 300 million Americans out of approximately 7 billion people in the world. Over one billion people on the planet live on less than one dollar a day. Americans spend more than that on coffee, soda pop, gum, or water. Not all four, just one of those luxury items on a daily basis. Fifty percent of the world, 3.5 billion people, live on less than $3 per day. Eighty percent live on less than $10 per day. Where we live, our minimum wage is just under $10 per hour, just over what eighty percent of the world labors all day for. Please note that when the rest of the world works an entire day, it is much longer than eight hours and they do not receive breaks, lunch hours, worker's compensation if they are injured, or unemployment insurance payments if they get laid off. 1.1 billion people in developing countries have inadequate access to a water supply; not clean water, a water supply. At my house we have clean, safe drinking water running out of five different rooms. For fresh clean, safe drinking water we only have to walk at most twenty steps whenever we feel the slightest bit of thirst. 2.6 billion people lack basic sanitation, a place to go to the bathroom. Guys, we are ridiculously, insanely, unbelievably wealthy.

Before the recent recession, the number one growing business in America was storage units, "bigger barns." We actually have a new psychological disorder that is making national news. This disorder even has its own reality show. "Hoarding". I don't want to make light of people's problems, but are we seriously so stuck that we can't control overspending and never letting go of "stuff"?

Over the past twenty years, Tina and I have remodeled two homes and built another. This built up a large amount of equity in our mortgage. Just before the real-estate market crashed, we leveraged all our equity on a property development. Many of our friends made buckets of money in real estate so we figured we could do the same. We were so looking forward to paying off our home, buying new cars, a new boat, and starting college funds for our kids. On paper it looked absolutely amazing, but the market crashed and we lost our entire investment. It has been one of the most difficult times we have ever been through. But, as we have walked out this journey, we have continued to remind ourselves that we loved each other and God before we had money, while we gained financial position love was easy, and now we have lost it what will we do? As we rebuild, we want to stay true to our commitments to God, each other, and to our integrity. We thank God everyday for our jobs and the fact that we live in an amazing country where we have so many unbelievable opportunities.

Many Christians are blaming the government and the sinful behavior of our country for the hard times we are in. Some claim it is the judgment of God. I think we as the Church need to take a deeper look at ourselves. Are we trapped by the love of money? Are we serving money? Are we unable to serve God because we are so busy serving our own debt? We need to stop blaming others and start apologizing, because we are just as guilty as anyone else. Organizationally, as well as individually, we have loved comfort and luxury. We have built personal and organizational empires while most of the world literally starves. We seem to have barns for barns.

I recently read "Radical" by Platt. In his book, he writes of a denominational newsletter that boasted of a five thousand dollar donation, "by the entire denomination" to the poor in another country. In the same publication, there was mention of just one of their churches that recently built a fifteen million dollar, luxury church for themselves! It would be very easy to mock this, but have we looked in the mirror lately?

This is the simplest, yet most difficult, perception to change

The answer is not that all true Christians will be richly blessed. In my opinion prosperity theology just doesn't hold water. Not in America and certainly not around the world. Likewise the answer is not to live a monastic lifestyle, avoiding money all together. One of my favorite authors, Erwin McManus, says it like this, "The opposite of greed is not nothing. The opposite of greed is generosity." Money is not the root of evil. Money can be a blessing, as well as, an obsession. Blessings help and obsessions destroy. The "Money Hungry" perception people believe of the church is such a simple fix. We just need to give generously. What? Not so easy is it? That is why I said simple not easy. I think this may quite possibly be one of the most difficult things we will ever do. Here is how God says it:

> *2 Corinthians 9:6-11 "Remember this: Whoever sows sparingly will also reap sparingly, and whoever sows generously will also reap generously. Each man should give what he has decided in his heart to give, not reluctantly or under compulsion, for God loves a cheerful giver. And God is able to make all grace abound to you, so that in all things at all times, having all that you need, you will abound in every good work. As it is written: 'He has freely scattered his gifts to the poor; his righteousness endures forever.' Now he who supplies seed to the sower and bread for food will also supply and increase your store of seed and will enlarge the harvest of your righteousness. **You will be made rich in every way so that you can be generous on every occasion**, and through us your generosity will result in thanksgiving to God." (NIV)(Bold added)*

God blesses us, so we can be generous. There is nothing wrong with having money or nice things. In fact, *we can't sow generously unless we have something to give*. In God's economy, it is better to give than to receive. Scripture teaches to be faithful with little and God will give us more. For too long, we have built empires out of our church facilities, while living in personal luxury, hoarding all we have unto ourselves. We need to find a balance. These verses assure us if we give generously, we will receive generously. Giving to *"get"* is not generosity; it's investment bartering, and God is not fooled with such selfishness.

Having money or nice things is not sinful or evil. Only you and God can judge whether you own your things or your things own you. Only you can judge whom you are serving. I realize that I love shiny, fast stuff. I should say enjoy, not love, but the truth is I think way too highly of stuff and I have to constantly monitor my heart when it comes to material possessions. If we, as organizations, set limits on how much stuff people can own or how big their bank accounts should be, we revert to behavioral modification and become the judge. The Holy Spirit will lead us as well as everyone else, if we will listen and follow. For this reason I am not suggesting hard limits. God will speak to you as you listen

The above passage says we will be enriched in every way, so we can be generous on every occasion. God wants to bless every part of your life: financial, emotional, physical, relational, spiritual, and mental. He wants us to have all we need, so on every occasion we can be generous to all. ***If we want to dispel the belief that the Church is greedy, we as Christian churches, as well as individuals, must be generous***.

Being blessed in every way, so we can be generous in every way includes time, energy, talents, forgiveness, tolerance, patience, friendship, and money. If you are financially strapped right now because of debt, job loss, or anything else, you can start by being generous with your time. Help someone with a talent you have. Be generous with forgiveness. Be generous with friendship, patience, tolerance, and kindness. Give yourself away and watch what God does.

In a practical money sense, if we are going to be generous with our money, we are going to have to learn how to manage our money so we have some to give away. Christians as well as non-Christians are declaring bankruptcy. Christians are drowning in an ocean of debt that is sucking the life out of them, robbing all their time, depleting their energy, and killing their joy.

In some ways it seems the recession is subsiding. Now is a great time to learn how to manage money better and get free from the trap of greed. There are many financial books and classes you can learn from. My wife and I recently went through Dave Ramsey's Financial Peace University. It gives practical steps in how to get out of debt, create a budget, and save money for the future. By the way, Dave, in the off chance you are reading this, we recently paid off our credit line that has had a balance for over four years. In addition we have snowballed our other debts and now only owe money on our house. One fifth of our five-month emergency fund is in the bank. We love being debt free. Thanks for the great advice Dave.

If Christians are going to be known for generosity, we are going to have to stop swimming in debt, "serving money," and start having money serve us.

Another direct indication of the condition of our heart when it comes to greed is tithing. A Tithe is giving the *first* ten percent of your income to God as an act of obedience. This act of obedience provides for the Church to reach their community and world. It is something God asks us to do with a cheerful attitude realizing that everything we have is directly from Him.

Of all the statistics out there, a high result computes less than twenty percent of Christians in America tithe. The richest people in the world are the most disobedient when it comes to money.

Most churches have a hard time paying their staff and keeping the lights on, let alone being generous to the world. Some have said if all the Christians in America tithed, the Church could eradicate world hunger. I am not sure if that can be proven, but I will say this: if we are obedient, God promises His blessing to be so large that we will not be able to contain it.

We must understand God does not consider our tithe generous; tithing is the first step in obedience, and generosity starts after we obey. (The Bible promises if we obey God in this area we will have all we need, and He will always take care of us.)

This has been my personal experience and I say to you exactly what I say to our church. I have no idea how much anyone gives. I don't want to know, because I fear I would think of you and treat you differently if I did. This is something that is between you and God, and He will never force you to do anything you don't want to do. I don't want you to feel guilty or compelled to give. As the scriptures say, each of us should give what we decide in our own hearts to give. God loves a cheerful giver!

This does not let the leaders in the Church off the hook. The Church, as an organization, must be generous, too. We need to stop rating our success by attendance, building designs, or anything else that makes us think we are great. What should make us feel great is having a sizeable percentage of our time and income going to serve the poor around the world and helping our communities. Is this even a category we highlight in our yearly report? I hope so. We should be asking a very important question every day. "If our church were to close its doors never to return, would anyone in our community who does not attend our church miss us? Would anybody say of us, "I wish that church was still there, they were such a help to our community"?

Questions:

1. Do you wish you had less debt so you could do more for God?
2. Do you think you may be caught in the trap of Greed?
3. Have you ever refinanced your home to pay for your consumer debt? How many times?
4. Have you taken any money management courses in the last five years?
5. Do you honor God with a tithe of your income?
6. Do you consider yourself generous?
7. Would God consider you generous?

8. What is your next step(s) in the area of money?

Chapter 3:   Judgmental

*Romans 2:1-4 "You, therefore, have no excuse, you who
pass judgment on someone else, for at whatever point you
judge another, you are condemning yourself, because you who
pass judgment do the same things. Now we know that God's
judgment against those who do such things is based on truth.
So when you, a mere human being, pass judgment on them and
yet do the same things, do you think you will escape God's
judgment? Or do you show contempt for the riches of his
kindness, forbearance and patience, not realizing that God's
kindness is intended to lead you to repentance?" (NIV)*

It was the summer between my fourth and fifth grade year
that I first heard about Jesus. My mom and dad sent me to the
coolest summer camp ever, complete with motorcycles, BB
Guns, bows and arrows, and swimming. It was everything a
boy could dream of. During one of the evening services, they
shared about Jesus and how He died on the cross and rose from
the grave to take away our sins. They explained that Jesus
would forgive us of every sin if we asked for forgiveness and
pray a very specific prayer. Once we did that, we would go to
Heaven when we died. The alternative was Hell. I had never
heard of Hell, but it didn't sound good to me, so I prayed the
prayer they called *the sinners prayer*.

My family was not a church going family at that time, so

when I got home, it was life as usual. My parents loved us kids and each other very much, but like many people, each of them brought some pretty heavy baggage to the marriage. Growing up in very dysfunctional alcoholic homes, my mom and dad had many unhealthy life patterns and habits. It seemed every weekend there was a party at our house and the more they drank the easier life was for us kids. From my perspective, it was totally cool and I aspired to be just like them.

I had no idea my parent's marriage was in danger. They had major struggles and the partying was just an attempt to numb the frustration and pain. When I was in the sixth grade, my mom went to a Woman's Aglow luncheon where she met Jesus in a very real way. Her entire countenance changed. She was always so agitated, fearful, and angry. But all that changed. One year later my dad came to Christ. Once he did, we had to attend church every week.

This began my journey in the Christian Church. Every week, I went to church, and every summer, I went to summer camp. I didn't attend church during my elementary years so when I was forced to go in the seventh grade, I had no idea how to act. It seemed that every Sunday I was in trouble with the church lady from Saturday Night Live. Sunday School teachers had no idea what to do with me. Over and over they talked about Heaven and Hell and Jesus giving His life so that I could be forgiven and not have to go to Hell. I prayed what they called the "sinners prayer" hundreds of times. It felt like I was a tiny little stick figure dangling over the pit of Hell on a very thin kite string.

It felt to me like all the Church wanted to do was take the fun out of life. Sit up straight, be quiet, pay attention, don't do this, don't do that or you will go straight to Hell. It took several years for me to truly understand John 10:10, *"The thief's (devil) purpose is to kill, rob, and destroy, but I (Jesus) have come so that you may have a rich and satisfying life."* *(NLT)* For a long time, the Church depressed me and made me feel like a total heathen, who was completely unacceptable unless I acted like them.

I did have some very meaningful encounters with God between the ages of twelve and seventeen, but many of them were induced by guilt and manipulation. I was terrified of going to Hell as week after week I was reminded of that possibility. It felt as if they put themselves in the judgment seat casting that eternal sentence on me every chance they could. But, in spite of the Church, I eventually understood and committed to a personal relationship with Jesus. When I did it was the greatest thing that has ever happened to me.

Before I gave my life to Jesus, I was one of the captains on the football team, had tons of friends, and went out most nights of the week. I had to be constantly surrounded by people, because I couldn't stand to be alone. My greatest need was to be liked and accepted. Whenever people weren't around to constantly affirm me, I felt desperately alone and completely void of purpose. The night I gave my life to Jesus, I went from feeling completely alone to having the greatest friend in the world. In fact, I have not felt alone since. I went from feeling shame and guilt to being free and happy. I went from feeling desperate and empty, to full and satisfied. It felt like I got a shower on the inside and was finally clean enough to be around God.

If Christianity is so great, why do people run from it?

When a person experiences the authentic salvation of Jesus, their life radically changes. Life comes alive feeling amazing and new. As they live out the virtues and values of scripture, their life heads in a direction they are proud of, and they start experiencing the blessings of living life the way God designed it to be lived.

I think this transformation is what causes people to want to share their faith. At first, most people just share the excitement and joy of how great they feel inside. Sharing your newfound joy and peace is pure and totally non-threatening or offensive. Most friends will celebrate your newfound joy as long as you aren't cramming it down their throats.

However, once a person settles into a faith community/church they can't help but take on the characteristics of that group. I don't want to judge all churches, so please don't think I am. With that said, the reason I am writing this book is because of my experience over the past thirty plus years, attending four different churches, working in five others, and talking with thousands of people who have shared their stories. From my personal experience and hearing hundreds more, it is very clear to me that many churches have been focused primarily on how people *should* and should *not behave.*

The main focus of the church has been on sin, restriction, and Hell, rather than forgiveness, freedom and abundant life. Churches tend to exert control over their people by coercing them with fear and judgment.

I have heard countless sermons comparing "the Church" (Christians) to "the world" (non-Christians). In these sermons, Christians were always portrayed as being far better people and far better off than those who live in the dark evil world heading straight to Hell. At church, we were told we must separate ourselves from the world, so we don't become tempted and fall back into sin.

The Church has cast its judgment on the entire world, literally creating an *us-and-them* culture. Not just us and them, but us against them. It is as if the only way the church can assure themselves of their salvation is to constantly prove other's damnation.

I don't think the Church has meant to do this, nor do I think the Church wants anyone to spend eternity in Hell. We have just gotten off track, sliding down a very fast and slippery slope of judging others. There is something inside us compelling us to answer the question of where we will go after we die. Even after we find Jesus, we have to reassure ourselves that we are in. We fall into the trap of performance-based, behavioral religion. We compare ourselves to people inside, as well as outside the Church; we don't cognitively think it through, but it seems we are driven to prove to ourselves we are saved.

The problem with humans deciding who goes to Heaven or

Hell is we become the judge. I was told how to dress, talk, and act. We weren't supposed to drink, smoke, or chew, or go with girls that do. I was told not to have non-Christian friends, because they would influence me to sin. The Church carefully scrutinized everything I did and said. I don't think the Church maliciously planned on being judgmental; in fact, most of us don't think we are at all, but is it possible that society's perception has become reality?

I am afraid our human nature is so flawed that we tend to want to control others and demand they believe what we believe and live the way we think they should live.

The Bible is our authority for living. Because we believe it to be totally true we use it as our gavel of judgment on all mankind. In our efforts to share the love of God with the world, we have taken a jaded and judgmental attitude in our approach. This has caused a great deal of emotional, spiritual, and relational stress between those who are inside the Church and those who are outside. This judgment has cast shame on people and has been clearly communicated through our words, body language, and voice tones. Again, this has not been a calculated and malicious plan, but this is how the people outside the church feel, so we must be willing to give it careful examination.

In this chapter, we will be apologizing for being judgmental. The Church has way overstepped its bounds casting judgment on mankind and demanding they submit to God and the church's expectations. God is the only one who has the authority to judge. In scripture, Jesus never demanded that anyone bow to His will. The whole premise and wonder of God is that He loves all people and gives every person free choice.

Free will

Could you imagine giving your kids absolute free will? When they are little, allowing them to choose what to eat for breakfast, lunch, and dinner? As they get older, giving them total freedom to attend school or not, freedom to date whenever and whomever they want, and freedom to use drugs or alcohol? When I picture free will, my mind almost instantly pictures the negative. But if it is truly free will, they also have the freedom to succeed and excel beyond all human recognition.

When it comes to our kids, we like the freedom to do good, but when it comes to the freedom for evil, we quickly apply the brakes. God doesn't! God gives all people freedom to believe whatever they want, act however they want, go wherever they want, say whatever they want, and be whoever they want to be. This is a huge objection people have towards God. Has this created a mess? Has this created pain? Has this created stress? Has this caused wars? Has this allowed for horrendous evil? The answer to all of these questions is a resounding… Yes! But what about the good side? Has this created amazing wonders? Has this created unbelievable joy? Has this created peace? Has this allowed for unbelievable acts of goodness? Again the answer is… Yes! If you have ever been married, you have most likely experienced all of these results with the same person.

God allows us to do good or bad. Mankind has done incredible evil and amazing good, all at the mercy of God.

Our problem with God's freedom is we want all the good and none of the bad. If we are totally honest, we might admit we wish God would control everyone else from doing evil, so our families could have the best possible lives imaginable. This is why the universe is not in our hands. This is why we are not God. This is why judging anyone is way, way, way out of bounds for humans. I wonder if the reason we exert so much control over people is because God does not? It just doesn't seem fair to let people destroy themselves or others. For this reason we try anything at our disposal to keep them from doing so. Controlling someone starts with judgment, and having control requires leverage. Christians use eternal damnation as leverage to scare and manipulate people through personally judging their lives. Why is God holding back His judgment? Maybe the answer is found in 2 Peter 3:8 & 9.

2 Peter 3:8-9 "Don't overlook the obvious here, friends. With God, one day is as good as a thousand years, a thousand years as a day. God isn't late with his promise as some measure lateness. He is restraining himself on account of you, holding back the End because he doesn't want anyone lost. He's giving everyone space and time to change." (MSG)

God created all people. It was His choice to give all of us free will. He gave us free will so we would not be robots forced to love Him, but children who genuinely adore everything He is. God is withholding His judgment, giving all people time and space to change. This is because He loves everyone. As the Creator of all things, who sees and hears all things, He is the only one qualified to make spiritual judgments. He has chosen to be patient. So patient that a day is like a thousand years and a thousand years is like a day. In that way of thinking, it has only been two days since the resurrection of Jesus. His eternal judgment might be a ways off. Since He is giving everyone time and space to change – grace and mercy to change, shouldn't we? When we judge, we look foolish because, as we point one finger at them, we have three more pointing straight back at ourselves.

Jesus said, "Do not judge others and you will not be judged." Jesus was not saying that God would not judge us. Every person will face judgment from the One who loves him or her more than anyone ever could. He is saying if we don't judge others, they won't judge us. He continues, "For you will be treated as you treat others." The obvious reason why there is so much animosity between those who are in the Church and those outside the Church is because those inside continue to pass judgment on those outside. No wonder those looking in from the outside are so angry.

I hope and pray with all my heart this book opens the door of relationship to people who have been hurt by the Church. In addition and even more so, I pray this book has lasting impact on the way Christians treat and interact with those who are outside the Church. For that to happen, we must be brutally honest with ourselves. We must be willing to see things from others' perspectives. We must understand who we are, who

God is, and where we fit into sharing His love with the rest of the world.

Is all judgment wrong?

The word judgment means: "A legal verdict. Obligation resulting from a verdict. A decision of a judge. Discernment or good sense. Opinion or act of making a statement." If we take off the suffix "-ment" at the end of the word, we are left with judge, which means: "Senior official in a court of law or somebody giving an informed opinion." Understanding the meaning of the word, I submit to you this statement. *Having good judgment* shows wisdom and saves you much heartache, *casting judgment* is foolish and causes incredible pain.

To judge something or someone, we must be in a position of authority or power. For example, if you have a problem with your car, you take it to a certified mechanic. He or she will give you an estimate based on their qualified judgment. They have the authority because of their knowledge and expertise. Judgment is incredibly simple when referring to inanimate objects. We all realize that Jesus was not talking about objects when He said do not judge.

When it comes to people, is there a difference between having good judgment and casting judgment? I believe so. We have a cardinal rule when it comes to our kids. They are not allowed to play at someone else's house unless we have met the parents and personally been to their home. The way this plays out is simple. If they are invited to a new friend's house, we go with them. My senses are on full alert the moment we pull in the driveway. If there are old rusty cars with jagged edges lying around the yard, that is clue number one. If we walk up the front steps and have to step over a hole in the front porch that needs repair, then go inside and see a very messy environment, including alcoholic beverages lying around and hypodermic needles on the coffee table, and we see things on the TV that kids should not be watching and a man sitting in his easy chair in nothing but his underwear cleaning a pistol; then my kids are not going to stay at that house. In fact, if it were that extreme, we would be leaving right away. Some people may say that is judgmental. I don't think so. This is called having good judgment, realizing it is not a safe place for kids to be. Likewise, when my girls are older and they start dating – say "twenty-five" (just kidding, wishful thinking and totally unrealistic), we will ask to meet the boy face-to-face and have a conversation with him. If he pulls up in a van that has a waterbed in the back, naked lady mud flaps, and a license plate that says, "born to be bad," their date will be canceled and we will have a much longer conversation. When that conversation is over, he will still not be taking my daughter anywhere.

Discernment is not the kind of judgment Jesus is talking about, nor the judgment we are apologizing for. This kind of judgment is wisdom and it saves you heartache. The kind of judgment we are apologizing for is being judgmental. Being judgmental involves judging a person's motive, character, and spiritual condition. When we look at a person, we have a very narrow window into their lives. At best, we can only observe the outside. We cannot see into their heart and discern their motives. We do not know their whole character; therefore, we can't judge their spiritual condition. Only God can do that.

Not trusting a person with your children or valuable possessions is having healthy boundaries. The difference is this: we did not judge the man sitting in his underwear, cleaning his pistol, as being stupid, crazy, filthy, piggish, selfish, or irresponsible. We also did not judge where he will spend eternity. We can't do that to his face, or behind his back after we leave. It is not our call. We simply do not allow our kids to play at that house because it is unsafe. If you are ever in a situation where your boundaries are being pushed, it is very difficult to have a caring, non-judgmental conversation about it. It is even harder to not make judgmental statements while talking to them or about them later.

We have a person who is close to us, who has a daughter the same age as one of our daughters. The girls love to play together. This person has been having a very hard time in her marriage. She had shared with us in confidence she does not feel physically safe with her husband. A month later, her daughter called and invited our daughter to spend the night. We said no, because we had other plans. We knew this invitation would be coming again very soon so we had a long conversation about it and decided we had to call her back and share with her that our busy schedule wasn't the only reason why we said no.

Our conversation was prefaced with how much we love

them and their kids, and how we love having their kids play with ours. We said we hope she does not feel like we are judging her or her husband, but we wanted to confirm that she felt unsafe. We had to let her know if she doesn't feel safe, then we don't feel safe either. For this reason and this reason only, we don't feel comfortable letting our daughter spend the night. We again affirmed we loved them, are very glad we are friends, and our kids could play together anytime she is present, or the kids are at our home. She handled it very well and we continue to have a good relationship. It is very hard to have boundaries and not cast judgment.

It becomes wrong when we go beyond creating healthy boundaries and start judging character, motives, or the condition of someone's heart and soul. It is so easy to skate over the fine line of having good judgment and condemning people's lives. In fact, I think I have crossed that line even from the pulpit. While I preached through this series, I apologized to our church, telling this exact story.

During a message this past year, I talked about one of my major pet peeves. I was a Youth Pastor for fifteen years. Throughout those years, I have had many parents say, "Johnny gave his life to Jesus when he was eight years old. He's a Christian, but he just isn't following Jesus right now." At this point, I usually just look at them like, "how is that possible?" They sense my frustration, so they often insert, "I mean, Johnny is a Christian, he's going to Heaven." From the pulpit, I then said, "Stop telling Johnny he is going to Heaven. Stop telling Johnny he can live like hell and still go to Heaven, because he prayed some magical prayer that doesn't exist in the Bible. The best thing that could happen to Johnny is if he could realize that he is not going to Heaven." When I said, "Stop telling Johnny he is going to Heaven." That is where I should have stopped.

We do not get to decide whether someone goes to Heaven or Hell, only God does. I don't even get to decide if my kids go to Heaven or Hell. If it was up to me, they are in, but it is not my decision. I went way over the line when I declared Johnny was not going to Heaven. I don't get to decide for my kids or anyone else. I apologized, because when I say something like that from the pulpit, it gives permission for everyone else to do the same. Sometimes we say things from the pulpit we don't mean to say, and then it becomes common practice in the lives of people in the Church. I am so sorry for encouraging people to judge others. I was way wrong.

Ever since I darkened the doors of a church, I have heard threats of Hell and eternal damnation. I have had people tell me if I keep acting in certain ways I will go there. We have had people do this to us and we have turned and done it to others. This next statement will be very offensive to some but the Bible is very clear about this. I know it is unpopular in our culture but according to scripture… People will go to Hell. If this is something that angers or upsets you I hope you realize that I am reporting what scripture says and I hope you will be open enough to look into it for yourself. With all that said, people do not get to decide who is in or who is out. Just as scripturally true is God loves every person and does not want anyone to endure that fate. He has gone out of His way to have a personal relationship with every person. We should never make judgments of people's character, motives, or eternal destination. Our judgment is wrong and it causes people to feel shame and disgust. No wonder so many people don't want to go to church.

How serious of a sin is judgment?

It seems that the Church likes to highlight sexual sin, murder, and abortion as the most deplorable acts of man. For some reason, it comes across like these are the most serious offenses a person can make and those who make them receive a more stern judgment. In the book of James 2:8-13, the Bible says that *"breaking one law is just as equal as breaking all the law"*. Missing the mark of holiness... misses. We are not graded on a curve, nor are we given extra points for barely missing. If we miss at all, we miss completely. Passing judgment is another way of breaking the law of God. He gave us the job of reconciler not judge. Breaking this law has very serious consequences.

Scripture makes it very clear at whatever point we pass judgment on others, God casts His judgment on us.

Romans 2:1-4 "You, therefore, have no excuse, you who pass judgment on someone else, for at whatever point you judge another, you are condemning yourself, because you who pass judgment do the same things. Now we know that God's

judgment against those who do such things is based on
truth. So when you, a mere human being, pass judgment on
them and yet do the same things, do you think you will escape
God's judgment? Or do you show contempt for the riches of his
kindness, forbearance and patience, not realizing that God's
kindness is intended to lead you to repentance?" (NIV)

I love to watch courtroom drama. What happens when a person in the courtroom stands up or simply shouts out their opinion? The judge says they must be quiet and if they don't, they will be held in "contempt". God is the judge; He and His son Jesus are the only ones who can judge. When we blurt out our opinion, even if it is fact from our point of view, it is called contempt - contempt against the living God. I love the mercy of God in my life; He is so patient, kind, and loving towards me even though I struggle with so many things. He doesn't violently slam the gavel on my life and end me because I am less than what He wants me to be. He doesn't call me stupid, idiot, moron, or anything that would make me feel like an inferior person. He lovingly directs and guides me. This is what He does for all mankind. He is patiently withholding His judgment, giving us time and space to change. He asks that we trust Him and allow Him to be the judge, while we bring people back together with Him.

We are not qualified to cast judgment, because we are flawed ourselves. Like we discussed in the first chapter, we look so hypocritical when we judge, because we have done so much wrong ourselves. I love verse four of this passage: *"It is his kindness that leads us to repentance."* We may have asked Jesus to forgive us out of a holy fear, but we chose to place our lives under His control because of his unbelievable kindness. The only way we could continue in His grace is through love. It was His kindness that won our hearts and devotion. It is His kindness that will win the rest of the world, too.

Judging a person's spiritual condition is not only out of line, it is cruel. Being around some Christians I get the feeling they are comforted by the thought of people they disagree with going to Hell. It actually seems to make them happy. We must understand God will not send anyone to Hell with a smile on His face. It will break His heart. If we want to truly reflect Him we must feel and show His brokenness for all mankind.

Sadly, many people think God hates them and can't wait to judge them and send them to Hell. We have focused so much attention on behavior, control and judgment that we have lost site of God's mercy and kindness. Because of our infatuation with behavior the Church in many ways, has become a giant daycare center struggling to control every little child of God.

Behavioral modification-ist

I think the reason so many people leave the Church is because they are fed up with having to conform to every fetish of the people-group they were trying to worship with. In many ways, the Church has become behavioral modification-ists instead of reconcilers of God's grace. We have become more concerned with how people dress, talk, and look than the brokenness in their lives. When I was growing up, our church used the word, "backslide" for when people started participating in sins they use to do before giving their lives to Christ. The Church would talk about temptation, and how we can be so easily tempted and fall away. They would blame it on being friends with people outside the Church. It was those outside influences that would cause people to stumble.

Romans 14:10-13 "You, then, why do you judge your brother or sister Or why do you treat them with contempt? For we will all stand before God's judgment seat. It is written: 'As surely as I live,' says the Lord, 'every knee will bow before me; every tongue will acknowledge God.' So then, each of us will give an account of ourselves to God. Therefore let us stop passing judgment on one another. Instead, make up your mind not to put any stumbling block or obstacle in the way of a brother or sister." (NIV)

This passage says to not judge each other. For so long, we have blamed temptation and outside influences on people stumbling or falling away. In this passage, we see *we* can be the greatest reason people stumble. It is not always sin and temptation that is the stumbling block, sometimes it is us. Many times, we are the repellant driving people away from God. I have talked to so many women who got pregnant out of wedlock and were shunned by their church, men and women who were shunned when they went through a divorce, and many others who felt shamed when they admitted struggling with their sexuality; not to mention, girls who were looked at and talked about like they were whores because they wore a skirt that was deemed too short, or God forbid, wore pants to church. Students have been thrown out for wearing a ball cap, saying a cuss word, or smoking cigarettes. The Christian Church is the only place I know where they kill their wounded.

James 2:12-13 "Speak and act as those who are going to be judged by the law that gives freedom, because judgment without mercy will be shown to anyone who has not been merciful. Mercy triumphs over judgment." (NIV)

I am so thankful for the mercy of God. Could you imagine if one of us was in charge? We are so fickle and so easily angered. Look at the destruction we cause with our weak, feeble power. Could you imagine what it would be like if we were all powerful? God is not angry, nor is He punishing people and trying to make them so miserable that they finally submit. We could not bear even the slightest bit of His wrath. We are living in the time of His grace and mercy. Please read this passage of scripture one more time very slowly.

2 Peter 3:8-9 "Don't overlook the obvious here, friends. With God, one day is as good as a thousand years, a thousand years as a day. God isn't late with his promise as some measure lateness. He is restraining himself on account of you, holding

*back the End because he doesn't want anyone lost. **He's
giving everyone space and time to change**." (MSG)*

We need to change what is important to us

When I preached this series at our church, I challenged
everyone with a very practical exercise. The idea was to get a
jar and place it in a prominent spot in your house. Give your
kids, your spouse, roommates, or even co-workers permission
to monitor whether you say something judgmental. Every time
someone catches you making a judgment, it costs you a
quarter. For the week of this exercise, their perception is
reality. It is based on their opinion if it was judgmental or not,
and you are not allowed to argue about it. When you put your
quarter in the jar, ask God to forgive you for being judgmental
and ask Him to help you stop the habit of judging. At the end
of the week, don't throw yourself an ice cream party. We don't
deserve ice cream, for this. Give the money to God; donate the
money to missions or an organization that helps people.

This challenge was right in the middle of the NFL playoffs,
so that week was much harder than I anticipated. During the
games, I noticed the commentator's judgments were often
directed at a player's character, not just their play on the field.
Funny how I notice other peoples' faults first. Then, I realized I
was doing the same thing as I talked with the guys about the
games. We had a blast trying to catch each other in judgment.
Because it cost a quarter for each offense, I held back many
things I wanted to say.

As the Pastor, I lead the staff of our church, so I asked them in advance if they would be up for the challenge, too. One thing we try to do every morning as a staff is spend a few minutes touching base, praying for each other, and addressing prayer requests from weekend services. Sometimes as we talk about our lives and people in our lives, we share different events and scenarios that happen. This often begins by asking for prayer. Sometimes as we explain what we are praying about, we cross the line and throw in our judgment. I am sure you can relate. We all have relatives or people in our lives that continue to make bad choices. As we share, we cross the line and share too much information, making it gossip. Then, we share our opinion of what they did, casting our judgment. Our disparaging comments make us guilty of slander. But, please remember, we are good Christians, so of course we pray for them. Ha, ha! This is no laughing matter, it is a very serious offense to God.

As I prepared the message that week, the Lord really convicted me of this. I couldn't read all those passages of scripture and simply shrug it off. This is something we have to change. We have some very bad habits and if we want to break a habit, we have to work at it. We have some flat out sin and we need to repent of it. Part of that repentance will include an apology to those we have judged.

We just went through the holiday season attending all kinds of family gatherings. I love getting together with my family; they are awesome people. I don't know about your family, but one thing the Lord is really convicting me of is that my family doesn't always have a lot to talk about, unless we are talking about someone who is not in the room. Gossip, judgment, and slander are a constant temptation.

We do this at church, at work, in our neighborhoods, at family gatherings, watching sports, and even to our spouse and children. This is one of the greatest objections people have to becoming a Christian. This is one of the biggest reasons people have left the Church, never to return. We need to realize that one of the biggest obstacles for our friends, neighbors, and co-workers coming to Jesus, might be us. We need to focus our attention on following God, not comparing ourselves to others. We are not closer to God because someone else is farther away. We must fight the temptation to feel better about ourselves, because we think we are better than someone else. We must stop trying to control people, and allow them to be directed and guided by the Holy Spirit. I have noticed I make judgments of peoples' motives, character, and spiritual condition all the time. We need God to convict us, we need to apologize, and we need to change.

Questions:
1. What bothers you most about other people?
2. Does your irritation come across as judgmental?
3. Who have you judged that you need to apologize to?
4. What has been your church experience?
5. How are you going to change this for others?

Chapter 4: Sexually Distorted

Genesis 2:21-25, "So the LORD God caused the man to fall into a deep sleep; and while he was sleeping, he took one of the man's ribs and closed up the place with flesh. Then the LORD God made a woman from the rib he had taken out of the man, and he brought her to the man. The man said, 'This is now bone of my bones and flesh of my flesh; she shall be called 'woman,' for she was taken out of man.' That is why a man leaves his father and mother and is united to his wife, and they will become one flesh. Adam and his wife were both naked, and they felt no shame." (NIV)

We darted off the school bus, hitting full sprint as soon as our feet touched the pavement. Trying desperately not to get soaked as we sprinted down our hill, through the neighbor's side yard, across the easement, through our backyard, and straight up the back steps. Three starving boys raid the refrigerator, then off to the basement to play Atari. No sign of any parents, so we were, as they say in the military, "speaking freely". Talking about girls, people at school, and anything else that came to mind. Swearing had never been allowed in our home. My mom had recently become a Christian and the standards were stiffening by the day.

Being in the sixth grade and all of eleven years old, I had a desperate need to constantly prove my masculinity and prove who was top dog. After dropping the "F" bomb several times, an unexpected voice called from above. I wish I could say it was God, but it was far scarier! "Matthew, could you please come upstairs?" I have no idea how my mom came in the house without me noticing, but she was there.

The humiliating trek up the stairwell seemed like climbing Hillary's step on Mt. Everest. It didn't help having my buddies and my younger brother laughing at me the whole way. As I walked the "eternal walk of shame", my mind was racing a mile a second trying to recall all the horrible words I may or may not have said. The worst thought of all was, "would she tell my dad when he got home". If there were any sharp objects in our stairwell, I may not be here today. Expecting the tongue-lashing of my life, she sat me down and calmly asked, "Matthew, do you know what %$#* means?" Without blinking an eye, she actually said the word. I tried not to laugh and replied, "I think so." We then proceeded to have a lengthy conversation about sex and the slang words used to describe it.

Our home was always a place of safety when it came to open dialogue about any and all issues, including sex. But that day it became much deeper and more open than ever. My parents had a very open and honest approach in teaching us about sex. From the very beginning we were taught we had arms, legs, fingers, toes, etc. Boys have a penis and girls have a vagina. We can show people our arms, legs, fingers (as long as it wasn't one all by itself), and toes, but it was inappropriate to share our more private parts. We never experienced the "Sex Talk." Sex was a topic that was an ongoing dialogue that happened naturally. It was always age appropriate and because of this, I have always felt free to talk to my mom and dad about anything.

When our family started attending church, we instantly had another influence on the subject of sex. At church, sex seemed dirty, wrong, and something that must be avoided. I was eleven years old when we started going to church. I knew babies were a result of sex, so I wondered how in the world our church leaders had children. At home, we had open and honest conversations about sex being God's gift to marriage between a husband and wife. At church, it seemed strictly taboo.

Distortion

I have entitled this chapter "Sexually Distorted" because in many ways the Church has been a terrible example of what God intended sex to be. Sex is God's idea! The Bible talks about sex a lot. Teaching about sex should not only occur at home, it should be a natural/"normal" subject in the Church. The devil has very successfully distorted sex, making it nasty and wrong. God didn't intend for sex to be dirty. He created it to be extremely pleasurable and an amazing gift that literally makes a husband and wife one flesh. There is nothing more pure and amazing than the gift of sex. For some reason, the Church has blushed, been ashamed of, and mishandled the subject of sex. We have seen in every denomination pastors, priests, board members, deacons, Sunday school teachers, youth leaders, and prominent people continue to be caught in sexual scandals, adultery, fornication, pornography, and everything else the devil has used to ruin the amazing gift God made.

***Distorted:** misleading, reconfigured from correct shape, and alteration from clarity.*

Our children are listening and watching our "every" move and so are people who are considering the claims of Christ. As a youth pastor, I have had to help several kids through very awkward situations where parents had affairs with other people in the Church, divorced their spouse, and wound up sitting on opposite sides of the church from each other. One time in a church I was Youth Pastor for two couples swapped spouses. They never could figure out why their kids thought church was a total joke.

Statistically speaking the Christian Church has the same divorce rate as people outside the Church. One Seattle newscasters said, if the Church could have a lower divorce rate than those outside the Church, he might consider listening to them. Amen, Mr. newscaster! If we want to represent the awesome name of Jesus, we must change this statistic.

There are many parents who have been faithful to each other and managed their sexuality in a very noble manner. With that said, many of those very same Christian parents, in their prudence, or lack of preparedness, have portrayed an attitude of shame and or embarrassment about this amazing gift from God. For example, when parents make up cute names for private parts because they are too embarrassed to say "penis" or "vagina" they send a message of shame about their children's sexual organs. When parents avoid sexual questions, lie, or blush, they send a message of secrecy and disgrace. When parents freak out on their teenagers because the subject of sex comes up, they push their kids away and exclude themselves from one of the most vital conversations teens need to have.

As parents, we should be trusted resources that have accurate and honest answers kids need. But for many people raised in the Church, they are merely perpetuating what they were taught – "Sexual Distortion." We not only owe an apology to those outside the Church, we owe it to those whom have entrusted us to teach them the Word of God.

Where did sex come from?

Sex was and still is God's idea. He created sex to be between a husband and wife inside the marriage covenant.

Genesis 2:21-25 "So the LORD God caused the man to fall into a deep sleep; and while he was sleeping, he took one of the man's ribs and closed up the place with flesh. Then the LORD God made a woman from the rib he had taken out of the man, and he brought her to the man. The man said, 'This is now bone of my bones and flesh of my flesh; she shall be called 'woman,' for she was taken out of man.' That is why a man leaves his father and mother and is united to his wife, and they will become one flesh. Adam and his wife were both naked, and they felt no shame." (NIV)

It is not good for us to be alone. All human beings have a desperate need for love. God truly shows His love and understanding of us in our sexuality. In our deep need for intimacy, God made a way for us to become one flesh with the one person with which we make a lifelong covenant.

The marriage relationship is absolutely amazing and sex is a very powerful closeness that celebrates unity and deepens intimacy between a husband and wife. The best way to describe sex is, "One Flesh." Don't be fooled by the word *flesh*. Sex is not just oneness of our flesh. Sex is oneness of heart, mind, and emotion. Sex even gives us a spiritual connection. The devil would like us to believe that sex is purely a physical act to give us pleasure. However, if sex were only a physical need, we would be no different than animals in heat. Sex is a very big deal! There is a level of intimacy shared between a husband and wife that cannot be achieved by anything else. Not that sex by itself is intimacy, but it is a very big part of it.

Sex is not only God's idea… Sex is supposed to be **incredibly pleasurable**. There is a book in the Bible called Song of Songs that describes a passionate sexual love between a husband and wife. The name, Song of Songs, is like saying the best of the best, the song of all songs. Since it is speaking of making love, it is saying the best lovemaking of all lovemaking. Here is a sample…

Song of Songs 4:9-16, "You have captured my heart, my treasure, my bride. You hold it hostage with one glance of your eyes, with a single jewel of your necklace. Your love delights me, my treasure, my bride. Your love is better than wine, your perfume more fragrant than spices. Your lips are as sweet as nectar, my bride. Honey and milk are under your tongue. Your clothes are scented like the cedars of Lebanon. You are my private garden, my treasure, my bride, a secluded spring, a hidden fountain. Your thighs shelter a paradise of pomegranates with rare spices—henna with nard, nard and saffron, fragrant calamus and cinnamon, with all the trees of frankincense, myrrh, and aloes, and every other lovely spice. You are a garden fountain, a well of fresh water streaming down from Lebanon's mountains." (NLT)

Yes, this is quoted right out of the Bible. This may not be the kind of poetry you enjoy, but clearly sex is something that is extremely pleasurable and something God delights in. Not only does the Bible speak of the delight of sex, simple logic would deduct that God designed us to have extreme sexual pleasure. Think about it. A kiss is a magical thing. God created our lips with incredibly softy tissue packing them full of very sensitive nerve endings. When our lips touch another, indescribable sensations rush through our entire being. If we move a little south of our lips we have other parts of our bodies that are even more sensitive. God could have very easily made our lips tough and our genitals simply for releasing bodily fluids. But He didn't. He is the God who not only created pleasure; He gives us the gift of giving our spouse incredible pleasure while we enjoy the same. Sex is God's idea and it is supposed to give unbelievable pleasure! This gift is for us to receive from and give to our spouse. It's not only okay; it's encouraged. To use a churchy term, can anyone shout, "AMEN!"

Why is the Church so weird about sex?

As we read in John 10:10, the devil wants to kill, rob, and destroy everything God meant for good and when it comes to sex, He has done a very good job. God made sex to be a wonderful gift of pleasure to be shared between a husband and wife, and the devil has perverted what God made sacred. The Church seems to be ashamed of what God has given because of the way the devil perverted it. *Titus 1:15 says, "To the pure, all things are pure." (NIV)* When my children were very little, they became curious about their body parts. Like most small children they asked questions.

There is no need to be ashamed of a penis, vagina, breasts or pectorals. They are part of our body. As children grow older and need to know more information, there is still no need to be ashamed to talk openly about sexual issues. Inside of marriage, sex is absolutely pure and totally God's idea. We can talk about these things without embarrassment because we are pure when we manage our sexuality the way God intends. If we as parents or church leaders are embarrassed or treat sex as if is dirty, secretive, or shameful, that is how people will manage sexuality in their lives.

The purity of sex has been stolen by the devil and it is time we take it back. Not only has the purity been stolen, so has the freedom and enjoyment. Great sex is derailed through false beliefs, misguided feelings, and mismanagement. False beliefs, misguided feelings, and mismanagement occur when we buy into sexual myths.

Three common myths about sex

Myth number one… Sex outside of marriage is okay. Fornication is the word used for sex outside of marriage. *1st Corinthians 6:18 in the King James says, "Flee fornication. Every sin that a man doeth is without the body; but he that committeth fornication sinneth against his own body."* In the NIV, the word *fornication* is interpreted *sexually immoral*. The NIV says it this way. *"Flee from sexual immorality. All other sins a man commits are outside the body, but he who sins sexually, sins against their own body."* There are dozens of passages of scripture condemning fornication in the King James and they have now been interpreted in modern English as sexual immorality. People ask me all the time where the Bible says that sex outside of marriage is sin. Sexual immorality and fornication are the same thing – "sex outside of marriage."

God did not set this standard to rob our fun. He set this standard because operating outside of it only brings temporary pleasure followed by great pain. It is so amazing how hard the devil works to get people to have sex before marriage. Then after they are wed, he does everything he can to keep them from the true enjoyment God intended.

Myth number two... pornography will help my arousal and sexual interest. Nothing can be further from the truth. Pornography is one of the major contributors to perversion. The strongest sexual organ we have is our mind. Pornography robs people from natural arousal. Viewing people who are young and often surgically enhanced in perfect makeup and special lighting is not reality. Viewing people doing disgusting things with multiple partners, same sex partners, and animals is what God calls detestable. If we allow our minds to live in that fantasy world, reality can lose its appeal altogether. Being in love and celebrating genuine love through marital sex is an extreme act of giving yourself away. Pornography is all about taking. It is about having a desire and fulfilling it instantly with no love or intimacy. The person in the picture, video, or computer screen is saying what everyone wants to hear. "I want you now!" The problem is they aren't real; they are a fantasy, a mirage. Once that mirage is acted upon, it always spins into shame and regret because a mirage never satisfies. As soon as you dive in, you are neck deep in sand. With no commitment or sacrifice, we become habitual takers. Taking can never bring fulfillment because taking is void of intimacy. Intimacy is the ultimate satisfaction and pleasure we are looking for in sex. God said it is not good for us to be alone. So, He gave us marriage, not lust.

Myth number three… I will be a better lover if I have multiple partners. I have had the opportunity of meeting with several married couples over the years to talk about their marital difficulties. I have never once had someone be grateful for their past sexual experiences before marriage. Most women feel tremendous regret and guilt. For many women, it literally makes them want to avoid sex altogether. In men, they often find their minds wandering during sex, not being able to erase past sexual encounters or images from their memory. This is one of the major reasons people who were sexually active before marriage stop having sex after they are married. If this has been an issue for you, I encourage you to go talk with a trusted pastor or counselor and start working through it. God designed sex to be a gift for you and your spouse. God wants you to know that He forgives your past and wants to set you free from all past hurts and shame. It is His desire for your marriage to be a wonderful love affair that is highly celebrated between you and your spouse.

Recognizing the traps.

I need to be incredibly blunt here. If you are a Christian, you must be the real deal! Especially when it comes to managing your sexuality. As Christ-followers, we represent the name of Jesus. Our children, as well as the rest of the world, are watching. We cannot afford any more sexual scandals, divorces, or sexual deprivation of any kind. Sexual sin is not something we fall into all at once. Sexual sin is cultivated in the secret places of our private world. The longer we live in secret, the deeper we get into trouble.

The first closet that must be exposed is pornography. If you are viewing pornography, your attitude towards the human sexuality is drastically skewed towards perversion. Pornography traps you in a prison of lust making you believe instant self-gratification is what people are to be **_"used"_** for. Pornography cheapens human sexuality and reduces humanity below that of the animal kingdom.

God created us to give ourselves away and truly love one person for the rest of our lives. When we self-sacrificially and unconditionally commit our love for a lifetime, we find the true intimacy and unbelievable sexual pleasure God designed. Pornography robs us of sexual pleasure while highjacking the love and intimacy we desperately crave.

Pornography is also chemically addictive in your brain. If you are stuck in a fantasy world and desperately want out, be the real deal and get help: go to a counselor, pastor or trusted friend.

Another trap begins in very innocent friendships we have with people outside our marriage. These friendships or co-workers become emotionally and later physically intimate. Companionship is a built in need in all of us. Even if our marriage is good, we can build affections towards people at work, church, the neighborhood, or anywhere we go. The Bible says to guard your heart for it is the wellspring of life. The Bible says to take every thought captive. The Bible says to run away from temptation. In our ministry environment, we have a very strict rule to never work alone with anyone of the opposite sex. My wife and I have always had a very strict rule of not being alone with anyone of the opposite sex, even if it is for work. I know this is not always possible especially in the marketplace, but we do need to be as careful as we can.

Most of the time, unhealthy relationships start as a simple crush. We notice the other person is attractive, we feel comfortable talking with them, and enjoy their company. As the crush escalates, we find ourselves feeling excited when we know we are going to see them making sure we look as good as we possibly can. Just being in their presence feels euphoric, almost intoxicating. As this affection grows, we find ourselves thinking about them more and more. Over time thoughts of physical interaction start creeping in. This can happen even if our marriage is going good, no wonder it happens so often when the marriage is fractured.

I highly recommend accountability partners to everyone. Pray for, and seek out, a trusted friend you can meet with on a regular basis for prayer and accountability. "Girls with girls and guys with guys." Guys and girls think and communicate very differently. Meeting with a trusted friend of the same sex allows you to share openly with a person who thinks like you. It is wonderful if you can share everything with your spouse, but I will be very honest. If my wife is struggling with an area of her thought life that has to do with being attracted to another guy, I don't think I could handle it. I trust her completely and if she is struggling with those thoughts I know she will do everything she can to honor God and me. A woman will understand where she is coming from and be able to walk her through those feelings far better than I can.

I meet with my accountability partner every Tuesday morning. We ask each other three specific questions, talk about life, and pray together. The questions we ask have been mutually agreed upon in advance. Accountability is not being in a place of authority over each other. Accountability is being willing to submit and answer honestly. Here are the questions we ask: 1. How is your thought life? 2. How is your marriage? 3. What are you studying in Scripture? Most of the time these questions are very easy to answer. However, the reason why I have made this meeting a major priority in my life is because sometimes they're not.

Unashamed

Sex is God's idea. Sex is absolutely one hundred percent pure when we live according to God's plan and managing our sexuality is a major part of our lives. Christian leaders and parents should not allow the devil to pervert human sexuality. We should be very open and honest every time the subject arises. We must be willing to bring the subject up and be intentional about teaching it.

Sexuality affects every person on the planet. For this reason, we must be teaching God's provisions for this amazing gift. In educating our congregations and individual families, we should always use correct terms and be age appropriate. If we blush, make up cute little names, try to avoid, condemn, or get flustered about human sexuality, we send a message that it is wrong. This causes a huge problem because all people are sexual beings and have an enormous desire to explore and understand their sexuality. If we don't provide pure direction, our congregations, as well as our children, will be left with having to discover it from those that are speaking the loudest. I am not ashamed to talk about sex from the pulpit or in any one of our ministries in the church. I am not and will not be ashamed to talk about sex with my kids.

My oldest child first asked us what sex was when she was in kindergarten. I will never forget that moment. We were sitting on our front porch on a beautiful spring day waiting for the bus to drop her off. Being in kindergarten comes with the privilege of the school bus stopping at every house. It was a beautiful Sunny afternoon and my wife and I were sitting on the front porch talking as we waited for her. As she ran up the driveway with her cute little pigtails, lugging her *hello kitty* backpack, I had one of those moments where your mind takes a mental photograph. Wow, my baby girl was in school and riding a bus all by herself. She sat down in between my wife and I and began sharing about her day. As our conversation grew, she very innocently asked, "Daddy, what's sex?" I felt another very profound moment upon us. In that moment, I knew I had a very important choice to make.

One of our major goals as parents is to create an open and honest environment where our kids can talk to us about anything. I was so blessed to have that in my family growing up and I really want my kids to have the same. But this was kindergarten. I wasn't looking for this conversation nor was I totally prepared for it at this time. But it was the question my baby girl needed answered. After asking her why she asked, I made a deal with my little girl. I said, "I am so glad you asked me that question. I want you to know that you can ask Daddy anything you want and I will always tell you the truth. I am going to tell you what sex is and I will answer any other questions you have, but you have to promise me that you won't tell your friends. Mommy and Daddy want you to know the truth, but not all your friends' parents feel the same way we do. Do you promise?" She said yes, so I said, "You know how boys have a penis and girls have a vagina?" she said, "yes." "Sex is when a man puts his penis inside a woman's vagina."

She sat there with her mouth wide open, trying to process this overwhelming information. She said, "But Dad, the kids on the bus talk about it like it's cool." I said, "I know honey, many of them have no idea what sex is, but some day you will understand." Another long open-mouthed pause. Then she tried to reiterate her struggle to understand, "But Dad, you know how they talk about rock stars like they are cool? That is how they talk about sex." I said, "I know honey." At that point our conversation moved on, but we revisited that conversation many times that month and we have had an ongoing dialogue about this topic for sixteen years and counting. I am so thankful that our kids talk to us about these issues. In fact, every time things like this come up, I feel incredibly privileged to be a trusted advisor in their lives. My wife and I count it one of the greatest privileges to be in on the conversations our kids want and need to have. The last thing we want is for them to learn about sexuality from other kids or distorted philosophies.

There are many wonderful books about how to talk to your kids about sex. I highly recommend studying as many as possible. Your kid's sexuality, as well as their future marriage, is depending on your efforts. In addition, the Church needs to stop blushing and get real. Kids are having sex as early as the fifth grade. Some even sooner. We better start addressing this subject and teach God's Word.

Homosexuality and Lesbianism

Before officially publishing this book I asked several trusted friends for their edits and comments. Many have asked, "What is your stance on homosexuality and lesbianism?" This is a major topic in our culture and one I do not feel I can duck in this chapter.

I first want to say that my opinion as a Pastor in the Christian church on this subject as well as all other biblical absolute subjects is formulated and based purely from God's word. When I say Biblical absolute I mean that the bible directly addresses the subject with absolute clarity. In the case of sex it is one of the clearest and most talked about topics.

With that said I do not think my opinion matters. What maters are how I respond to and treat my fellowman. Since I have made scripture the number one authority in my life I am bound to reporting it as it is. I also do my very best to apply all of it in my daily life.

Scripture is very clear that sex is meant to be between a man and woman in the context of marriage. It is also very clear that homosexuality and lesbian behavior is sin. Here are just a few scriptures you can look up. (Leviticus 18:22, Romans 1:18-32, 1 Corinthians 6:9-10)

The very sad and twisted distortion is how the church has responded to sexual sin. "Heterosexual as well as homosexual" We often treat sexual sin, especially homosexuality and lesbianism, as it is the very worst thing a person can do. We look down upon, shame, judge, and cast out. We even call people names, slander them, and threaten them with eternal damnation in Hell. (As if that is our judgment to make.) – "Not!" Sexual sin has different consequences in the natural world than murder, gossip, greed, gluttony, etc. However in the spiritual realm it is exactly the same. Sin separates us from God and brings us pain. This is why God hates sin and gave his one and only son to free us from sin.

I am so sorry for how the church has treated the homosexual and lesbian community. They are people created by God whom God loves very much. So much that he gave his one and only son for them, just as much as he did for me or anyone else in the world. (John 3:16) We have been so arrogant, hateful, mean, and flat out wrong in our response. We have sinned in this area and we should be very sorry. I am!

We're sorry.

In addition I am so sorry for the sexual abuse, adultery, fornication, and perversions that have gone on in the Church. It is utterly shameful!

I am so sorry for the hatred and condemnation that has been shown to the homosexual and lesbian community. It is nothing but hatred, judgment, and **<u>fear</u>**. It is un-Christ like and incredibly wrong.

I am so sorry for the distortion of sexuality in the church. Many people have been robbed of their sexuality because of misguided, distorted, and overzealous prudence.

If you have been a victim of any kind of sexual abuse, I am very sorry and so is God. That was never God's plan and I pray you can become healed from your past wounds.

If you are presently being abused by anyone, including someone in the Church, please report the abuse to the police right away. No acceptations – turn them in. God always has and always will allow us to suffer the consequences and reap the rewards of our behavior. ***TURN THEM INTO THE POLICE!***

Questions:

1. How did your church teach about human sexuality when you were growing up?
2. How does your church teach about sexuality now?
3. How did your parents approach the subject of human sexuality?
4. How are you approaching the subject of human sexuality in your family?
5. Do you have some traps you need to get away from?

Chapter 5:   Political

*Romans 13:1-2 "Let everyone be subject to the governing authorities, for **there is no authority except that which God has established. The authorities that exist have been established by God.** <u>Consequently, whoever rebels against the authority is rebelling against what God has instituted, and those who do so will bring judgment on themselves.</u>" (NIV)*
(Emphasis added)

Thus far, we have apologized for being hypocritical, money hungry, judgmental, and sexually distorted. Saying or even thinking about these issues evokes no redeemable qualities. In this chapter, we are going to uncover ways we have been political. Most people hear the word *political* through a filter of many negative messages and experiences. Many people who have left the Church sight politics as one of the major contributing factors for their departure. Both internally as well as externally the Church has been a political minefield. Before we launch into this topic, it is important to understand what the word *political* means.

Political: Concerned with party politics, concerned with government, concerned with power, and pragmatic.
Synonyms for political include: following, taking sides, biased, opinionated

Are there any positive attributes to being political?

Speaking in the purest sense of the word, there may be a few redeemable qualities to this expression. First, all people should have concern with government. If you are an upstanding citizen in the United States you have the privilege to vote. After thoroughly studying the issues and gaining clear understanding for what each candidate stands for, our one vote should be cast. Living in a free country affords us the amazing opportunity to privately vote our personal values and convictions. What a tragic waste to abstain from such an overwhelming privilege, which was paid for at the highest price. Second, the Church as an organization, as well as individuals, should be concerned about, recognize, pray for, and support whoever is elected to office. Third, because we follow God, whom we profess to be the all powerful, almighty God, we should be at total peace no matter who is in office because we know God is leading our country the way he wants it to go. If we were to remain true to these convictions, not overstepping our bounds by enacting force or manipulation, we might possibly avoid the negative perceptions of being politically driven. Likewise, if we followed the instruction of scripture on how to relate to each other, we might avoid the internal political accusations as well.

In addition, there may be some positive expressions when it comes to the synonyms for being political. We do follow someone... Jesus. We have taken sides... Jesus. We are biased... We believe and follow scripture. Another word describing political is the word pragmatic.

Pragmatic: Concerned with practical results, and learning lessons from history.
Synonyms for pragmatic include: hardnosed, sensible, matter-of-fact, no-nonsense, realistic, practical, hardheaded

Again, from a positive perspective, we should learn from the past; we have made many mistakes and scripture is loaded with all kinds of valuable history lessons. Being sensible, realistic, practical, and resolved are all positive attributes as well.

There are some positive angles to view politics from, however, there is also a gigantic downside or "Dark Side".

The Dark Side

Sam Rima wrote an excellent book about leadership called *Overcoming The Dark Side of Leadership*. The premise of this book is all people have leadership gifts and strengths. As those strengths stand tall in the sun, their brilliance radiates to all those standing on the sunny side of those strengths. Remember the first time you noticed your shadow while standing in the sun? As a young boy, I was absolutely enamored by the immense mass that mimicked my every move on the dark side of the sidewalk. This is the dark side, the shadow. Lurking in the shadows of our strengths are the weaknesses of what is celebrated and admired.

All strengths have a dark side, especially when they are overplayed. For example, I am a type A, self-motivated, internally driven person. I almost always know what I want and am able to articulate it very clearly. I don't fear confrontation and usually think fast on my feet in most conversations. From the moment Tina and I met, she immediately recognized these qualities, which are a large reason for her attraction to me. Like most married couples, opposites attract. Tina is very easy-going, gets along with everyone, and rarely ever says something she has not thoroughly thought through. From the moment we met I fell head over heals in love with her and she with me. We loved that we each have strengths the other doesn't possess.

Then, we had our first major disagreement. In a disagreement, she feels like I am an overbearing lion hunting her down and pouncing on her every weakness. I feel like she runs and hides the moment we start to disagree. We have been together just over twenty-six years now. Through a lot of hard work, we have made these gifts work. Why is it work, because we all have a dark side to our strengths. Through honest and open self-discovery, we can overcome them.

If the Church has any positive attributes when it comes to being political, these positives represent strengths that stand tall in the sun. However, lurking in the shadows of our strengths is an overarching attitude, tone, look, and body language that have generated a horrendously negative vibe between the Church and the rest of the world.

These destructive character flaws are described clearly in

one word that is a synonym for political: ***opinionated***!

Having an opinion is neither good nor bad. In fact, having an opinion is part of being human. However, *"being opinionated"* commutates forceful, emphatic, and absolute positions that polarize relationships. Sharing an opinion isn't the problem. How we communicate, propagate, and advance our opinions is how we have earned the negative connotation of being "political."

Over the years, I have talked with many people who were totally sold-out for God, as well as heavily involved in their church. They became causalities in the war of opinion. The church seems to have an opinion about everything.

Our leading strength may be our greatest weakness

The Christian Church believes there is only One, True, Living God. We believe Jesus Christ is the only way to Heaven, because He paid the debt of death for all mankind when He died on the cross. We believe Jesus rose from the grave, conquering sin and death, and that all people can be reconciled to God through His sacrifice. We believe the Bible is the infallible Word of God and it is the ultimate authority over our lives. Another way of saying this is… We are totally convinced we have "The Truth". Jesus said He is the Way, the Truth and the Life *(John 14:6)*. The foundation of who we are is "The Truth" of God. This is an enormous strength. Unfortunately, this amazing strength, (overplayed), has become a gigantic "dark side" because of the way we communicate it.

This strength has been overplayed through expressions of force, threats, judgment, anger, sarcasm, and disparagement. Our attitude is often polarizing instead of reconciling. We come across as opinionated rather than caring. As a result new friendships fail to develop while existing ones erode until they are completely destroyed. Jesus gave us the task of reconciling the world to God, yet in many ways, we have accomplished the exact opposite.

Right

Human beings love to find *the* answer. We love being right. When we think we are right, we feel empowered, bold, and resolute. The Bible says, when a person discovers the truth of Christ and begins a personal relationship with Him, the Holy Spirit lives inside them. This is a power they understand intellectually, as well as feel deep within their soul. Having the power of God transforming your life from the inside out is an incredibly powerful experience. This sense of power, coupled with biblical truth, is something we must be aware of and never misuse by forcing truth upon other people. God loves all people and has given all of us grace and free will. God never forces us to do anything. Today, Christians are known as being some of the most forceful, emphatic, and polarizing people in the world.

When we believe we are right, we tend to think we are the only ones with the corner on "The truth". Because we have "The Truth", no one else's thoughts or opinions deserve to be heard. How we communicate is everything. For example, if I say, "I believe the Bible is the Word of God." That is my personal opinion. I may even share the result of that opinion in my life and say, "Because I believe the Bible is the Word of God, I accept it as the supreme authority over (my) life." Sharing this as my personal opinion usually comes across as non-threatening conversation.

But, if I say, "The Bible *is* the Word of God, and it *is* the final authority over all people," then this is a bold declaration that will instantly polarize relationships. Once the two sides separate, they become political factions, build their cases, and fight for supreme position. A very common mistake is to think if something is true, then it doesn't matter how we communicate it. Some people act as if it doesn't matter how truth is presented, so long as it is "The Truth."

Faith – "Sure of what we hope for, certain of what we do not see"

When it comes to sharing scriptural beliefs, we must realize we are sharing beliefs based on faith. There is very strong evidence for the authenticity of scripture, but no matter how we slice it, our beliefs are based on faith, and faith cannot be proven. The Bible says, "Faith is being sure of what we hope for and certain of what we do not see." Hebrews 11:1 (NIV)

I can say Jesus is God's one and only Son, but I can't prove it like I can by saying Sam is Jon's son. If I say Sam is Jon's son, I simply go ask Jon and Sam to verify the truthfulness of the statement. If you are still not convinced, we can have a DNA test done to give absolute certainty.

Things within our concrete world can be factual, but faith in a God we can't touch or see, simply remains faith. We can't prove Jesus is God's one and only Son until we go to Heaven and see for ourselves. Once we are there, we can't come back. Likewise, we can't prove creation because we are unable to observe or recreate it. No matter what we believe about the beginning of life it is a belief of faith. As Christ-followers, we share our faith: what we believe to be true because of what we have experienced in our hearts. Many churches and Christians have a very negative attitude towards people who choose not to believe the same things they believe. This attitude is very obvious and comes across as anything but loving.

Presentation

As Christ-followers, we live in relationship with God through faith. We must recognize and respect that many people don't have our same faith. In fact, most people in the world don't have the baseline of belief in scripture we have. This reality requires patience, tact, and tolerance of others.

Proverbs 15:1 "A gentle answer deflects anger, but harsh words make tempers flare." (NLT)
1 Peter 3:15-16 "But in your hearts revere Christ as Lord. Always be prepared to give an answer to everyone who asks you to give the reason for the hope that you have. But do this

*with **<u>gentleness and respect</u>**, keeping a clear conscience,*
so that those who speak maliciously against your good
behavior in Christ may be ashamed of their slander." (NIV)
(Emphasis added)

These verses are very difficult to heed when dealing with someone who is hostile towards faith. We must realize the reasons many people are hostile towards faith come from vast and complex issues. As I have built genuine friendships with people outside the Church and allow them to share their personal stories, it is overwhelmingly obvious that many people have not experienced respectful, loving, and gentle presentations of people sharing their faith. Tragically, it has been just the opposite.

Many people inside, as well as outside the Church have experienced Christians cramming the love of God down their throats. This attitude is communicated one-on-one, through many Christian TV ministries, and arrogantly blasted from pulpits in churches of all sizes.

People feel attacked by love.

Give that statement some thought. Does this make any sense at all? As Christ-followers we are commanded to love and befriend all people. In addition we are instructed to make every attempt to live at peace with everyone. In many ways the Church feels like a political faction that is flat out arrogant and rude. We are the ones who drew lines of demarcation in the sand. We have been extremely un-Christ-like when we have said, "turn or burn". We have made all people who question our beliefs or refuse to bow their knee, enemies rather than friends. We are supposed to be reconciling relationships, not tearing them apart.

Romans 12:18 "If it is possible, as far as it depends on you, live at peace with everyone." (NIV)

We appear to be a political faction in our faith communities, because we have tried to force our opinions and beliefs on people who do not hold the same convictions we have. Many Christian leaders are defensive, purposefully pitting themselves and their churches against society in an attempt to honor God. Many Christians try to police and enforce their moral beliefs and convictions on the rest of society. Professing Christians have yelled at the top of their lungs hateful, hurtful, profane, and disgusting things towards the people who disagree with them. We have provoked their anger and now there seems to be an all-out war between liberals and conservatives. It's a total failure on our part that two terms even exist. Some have even become physically violent. On each side, the political agendas are totally amped up and the battle is raging.

The Church seems to blame the Government

I can't remember a time when the two main parties of

government have been as polarized as they are today. The Republican Party has snuggled up to the Church and the Democratic Party to the more liberal agenda. The news stations know how to sell their product, so we now have entire news networks dedicated to one side or the other. The slanderous news allegations, commercials, webcasts, emails, and billboards are the worst I have ever seen. It appears the only reason to vote for one politician over another is because they are not as big a dirt bag as their opponent.

Whatever happened to making promises for what you will do if elected to office, and then being accountable for the promises you made? Both sides are equally slimy in their accusations and neither seems to care about anything but being elected and keeping their paycheck.

Society swallows these tactics hook, line, and sinker because we love to know whom to blame. For many years, the Church has attempted to use national government to advance our agenda. For the past fifty years things haven't gone as favorably as we like, so we use government as a scapegoat for all the evils in our country. Having someone to blame feels good, but I fear all we have done is abdicate our own personal responsibility.

The United States Government is a republic that has been designed to be of the people, by the people, and for the people. This means the people vote in the candidates they want. Another way to say this is *the people in leadership are the people "the majority of the people" want.*

Many Christian churches have declared their allegiance to

one party or the other. This has caused division in the individual church bodies, as well as the national Church as a whole. When talking about politics, some Christians act shocked and appalled if someone declares their allegiance to Christ, while at the same time declaring their allegiance to the political party they disagree with.

Recently, I was talking to a very bitter and angry older man. As we spoke his face grew a dark shade of red. With forceful tone and body language, he ridiculously bolstered, "a person can't be a Christian and a democrat at the same time!" I was absolutely shocked that a professing Christian would be so reckless in disobeying the Word of God by judging another person's spiritual condition based on how that person votes. I tried to engage in the conversation, but his position became more belligerent as we continued. Unlike this man, many Christians are wise enough not to say things like that out loud, but it sure seems by the way they slander others, they are thinking it. I have seen and heard professing Christians curse, slander, yell, and even become violent towards those they disagree with.

The majority of Christian churches were walking on air when a republican, who is a professing Christian, was elected to the presidency. Many Christians strutted around like proud peacocks because they not only elected a Christian president, but in addition the Republican Party had the majority control of both the house and the senate. They were completely convinced the Christian agenda would radically advance, and laws they oppose would be overturned, causing our country to become known as a Christian nation once again.

In many ways, the Church is putting their faith and trust in the government to bring about Biblical righteousness in our country. It's as if the Church is advocating governmental control over people's free right to choose whom they will worship.

I am not sure if they realize it or not, but that position says "if people won't believe what we believe and live up to the standards we want them to live up to, then the government should force them to do it because that is what we want."

Yes, we believe the Bible is God's Word, and yes, we believe it is the authority of our lives, but we must recognize the majority of the people in our country do not share our beliefs. Do we really want the government mandating that people live up to Christian standards? Before you answer that, you might ask yourself if you want the government mandating people live up to Muslim, Hindu, Buddhist, Bahia, or any other religion. The founding fathers were brilliant when they set up our nation to be a free nation. Do we really want to take that freedom away?

In the last two elections, the power shifted to the democratic side and a great portion of the Church has been shouting at the top of their lungs, slandering leadership, and running in fear throughout the whole process. The Church seems to be blaming the side they are against for all our country's problems.

Allow me some latitude while I use an older law as an example. In 1962, the Supreme Court ruled that government employees could no longer force all students to recite a prayer as they began each school day. From that ruling, there have been many cases that have brought about the evolution of the separation of church and state laws. The separation of church and state laws make it so no teacher or any other governmental official can impose any religious acts on anyone. This means teachers and school administrators cannot lead prayer or any other religious activities. This does *not* mean students can't pray. Students can pray as much as they want, to whomever they want, for as long as they want, so long as they are not being disruptive or forcing themselves on others.

Since 1962, the Church has been ranting that the government removed prayer from school. I was a youth pastor for fifteen years. Over those years, I spent countless hours on public school campuses. I hereby testify, kids can pray in school. Kids can even lead Bible studies under the equal access law that states if their school allows for any type of extra curricular club to meet on campus, then they must allow all clubs. Kids can pray all they want. Many Christian kids have been convinced by their parents, and or their church leaders, they are breaking the law if they pray at school. That is not true, kids can pray at school! Many kids are praying on campuses all over America every day.

Another example that makes some Christians go absolutely crazy is Rowe v. Wade. Please be patient with me on this. The reason people get abortions is because they want to, not because the government said it's okay. People were getting abortions long before the government passed a law making it legal to do so. We can't make the government the scapegoat for abortion. The government made it legal, thus making it far more available and easier for people to access. I don't agree with abortion personally, but I must admit there is one good part of this legalization: it is much safer... Safer for the mothers not the babies...

Please don't get me wrong; I am not for abortion at all. I believe with all my heart God is the creator of human life. A huge portion of that creation is done inside the mother's womb and I believe we are just as responsible for the care of His children in the womb as we are out of the womb.

With that said, I am very careful how I talk about this subject, because many women were led to believe that an abortion is a simple procedure removing a fetus from their body. Like having a wart removed. They were not educated on all the facts. The fetus inside them is a living, developing baby that she has an emotional, physical, and relational connection to. After having the abortion she was not prepared to deal with all the traumatic feelings that followed. They do not need to hear they are a murderer, nor should we blame the government for this evil. If the government is the blame or the answer, we abdicate our responsibility of spreading the righteousness of God.

A free government should not dictate or mandate moral and spiritual values. It is tragic and sad that laws give freedom to do things the Bible clearly teaches are morally and ethically wrong. We are given the freedom to cast our vote along with every other person.

It is very hard to watch laws take away the Christian influence the Church had when our country was founded. With that said, it is not the government's fault people don't want anything to do with the Church, following Jesus, or Biblical ethics and values. The majority of the voters in our country elected the people they wanted in office based on the moral ethics, values, and principles they adhere to. This is a scary time for me because we are living through the time period where our country is losing its Biblical moral compass. It is scary to think what it will be like for my children and grandchildren and it is scary to know that there are tragic consequences for not following God.

We must ask ourselves why the country has lost its Biblical moral compass and stop blaming the government. The Church is supposed to bring the love and righteousness of God to the world in a loving, giving, serving, and self-sacrificial way. This builds a bridge of friendship, allowing the Holy Spirit to bring true-life transformation into the deepest core of a person's soul. If we rely on the Government to mandate laws and policies to make people pray or behave the way we think they should, we are not only abdicating our responsibility to transform the world, we are advocating governmental control. Our responsibility is to reach the world with the love of God and let them experience true heart transformation. We have polarized ourselves from people outside the Church and created an enemy where we should have been building a friendship.

Deliberate separation

During the holiness movement era, the Church interpreted 2 Corinthians 6:17 where it says, "Come out from them and be separate" (NIV) as "Come out and be *separated*." We separated ourselves from the world by building our own schools and elaborate church facilities where we could educate and entertain Christians in every way possible. Our kids no longer have to go to a school that doesn't publicly pray and we don't have to go to non-Christian concerts, or non-Christian gyms. Churches have turned into Christian event centers where Christians can huddle together and stay safe/insulated from society. We even created exclusive systems so our people would only use other Christians for repairs and services. It has become so sick that some people wont even go on a cruise for vacation unless it is a "Christian cruise". We created our own sub-culture, and treated people who were outside the Church like they had a terrible infectious disease we had to stay away from. We moved out of the world and the world couldn't care less. We have lost all influence in the world because we are no longer living there.

The word separate does not mean separated. Separated is all about proximity. The word separate is about difference. In a world that lies, cheats, and steals, we should be so peculiar because we are honest, fair, and generous. We are supposed to be peculiar, different, "separate". This is why Jesus prayed we would be in the world but not of the world. (John 17). He has actually sent us to the world. We moved out and nobody cared. In fact they are all the more glad if we just stayed away. We must move back. We must be peculiar. We must be full of love, grace, and mercy. We must bring the love of God to our world, not run away from them because they might infect us.

The government will change because of the people who elect them. Right now the majority of our country does not want to follow biblical values. We can't blame the government. We must blame ourselves.

Political with each other

We are not only political with people outside the church; we are incredibly political with each other. Political factions within the church, like; those who want the walls brown and those who want them to be blue, those who want the music led by a piano and those who prefer guitar, and those who think we should dress up and those who go for a more casual approach. Each opinion couches their arguments in scripture they twist to back their position. As they battle innocent bystanders are killed in the crossfire. Jesus said, "they will know we are His disciples by our love for one another". (John 13:35 NIV)

Then there are the people who take it upon themselves to be the sin police. In scripture, there are biblical absolutes such as theft: "Thou shall not steal." Stealing is never okay, no matter what. If someone is caught stealing, yet calls himself a Christian and attends church, you can be sure they are going to hear from the church people about how they are not suppose to steal. In fact, there are many of teachings on biblical absolutes. If someone is breaking a biblical absolute, it is not uncommon to see him or her be confronted by people in the congregation. Often they become a spectacle of conversation in gossip circles all around that faith community. Friends of the person committing the alleged infraction come to their aid, making excuses and or defense. Political factions form on both sides and Christians fight to the death: the death of a person's faith and the death of the Christian witness for Jesus.

Today there are some Christian denominations that have chosen to move away from some of the "politically incorrect" biblical absolutes. These views or setting aside of scripture, have brought insurmountable disagreement. As people disagree, they talk with their friends, gossip and slander around the church, scream at each other in business meetings, and complain to anyone who will listen. These conversations may not be politically charged from inception, but the longer they fester, the grater momentum political factions generate. Breaking biblical absolutes are wrong; however, publically fighting with each other and forcing our agenda is *not* the correct way to handle the situation. Relationships have been destroyed and people are casualties in the war of politics within the local church.

Biblical absolutes are extremely difficult issues because the Church embraces scripture as their absolute right and wrong. Choosing to go against scripture is choosing to go against God's direction forces people to choose whom/what they will follow.

Unfortunately, enforcing biblical absolutes is not the leading reason why so many people continue to be hurt by the

Church. We have been political when it comes to our traditions, ministry styles, and personal preferences. I know of many churches that split when they stopped singing out of the hymnals and put the words of choruses on the wall using an overhead projector. When those same churches stopped using overheads and transitioned to computer-generated images through a projector, they split again. Churches split when they replaced the pews with chairs, started serving coffee, or used different musical instruments. Churches have split over the color of the carpet. If traditions aren't enough, there are the self-imposed moral positions of each individual local church. People have been shunned for wearing different kinds of clothes, going to movies, smoking, playing cards, drinking alcohol, wearing hats, and hundreds of other behavioral conformist mandates.

When people disagree, they often spread their disgust amongst their friends. This is usually framed in the context of asking for prayer and wisdom. As they talk, alliances are formed, political factions arise and people groups attempt to enforce their agenda. We use words like, "I feel like God is saying..." "Scripture clearly says..." "Thus sayeth the Lord!" We bring in many examples to help paint a more dramatic affect. Our analogies depict one side as "all evil", and the other as "all good". We quote scripture emphasizing our rightness. Sometimes it is in context and others it is blatantly out. In these scenarios we like to think people are arguing with God Himself rather than just human opinion. Therefore they must bow to our beliefs because The Almighty has spoken. Christians have muscled out pastors, deacons, elders, trustees, long-time members, and even people who are brand new to the faith.

As these verbal explosions thunder through the church, people are caught in the storm of emotion. How many millions of people have to be blown out of the Church before we are willing to change? Are we even willing to admit we are wrong? Have we convinced ourselves people leave the faith because they are weak, can't handle temptation, and run away because they prefer a life of sin? For some, I am sure this might be the case, but as I have listened to the stories, I am convinced Christians might be the greatest stumbling block there is on the pathway of people finding and relating to Jesus.

Are we a lost cause?

There is a tremendous amount of friction between those inside the Church and those outside. Truth be told, there is an enormous amount of friction between those who are the most regular attendees. One of my favorite sayings is "Where there is friction, there is traction." If you have ever been to a drag race, you may recall, before each race begins, each car always does a giant burnout. The burnout is not to showcase their power. The burnout is essential for the maximization of their power. The reason for the burnout is to heat up the tires. Friction creates traction! There is an unbelievable amount of friction between those who are in the Church and those who are not.

One of the major reasons for this book is to apologize for

all the friction we bring to this relationship. We have blown it in many ways and created massive unneeded friction. The good news is traction is maximized in the presence of friction. If we are willing to humble ourselves and make some critical adjustments, we can hopefully salvage these severed relationships and bring reconciliation between the Church and society. Our humility can be the first step in reconciling society to God.

What's our Job?

Let's start by understanding the fundamental roles God has assigned. The ministry of conviction was assigned to the Holy Spirit. The Holy Spirit will convict the world of sin, guide people into truth, and be our ever-present counselor, and teacher. The ministry of judgment is assigned to Jesus. Jesus is the name above all names that sits firmly on the throne and will judge the world at the end of the age.

Until the Day of Judgment, we are living in the time of God's mercy and grace. The followers of Jesus are given the ministry of reconciliation. We are not supposed to convict people of sin; we can't anyway, all we can produce is guilt and shame. We do not possess the knowledge, wisdom, or perspective to cast a just judgment in the first place. Only God can. We are supposed to love all people and encourage, build-up, and point them to the unconditional love of Christ.

True Friendships

I want to give use an analogy to help us understand how critical this is. Before I do, I want to be clear this analogy breaks down very quickly. The only thing a Christ-follower benefits from sharing their faith is the joy of partnering with Jesus in His creation and seeing people's lives become better on earth coupled with the peace of knowing they will spend eternity in Heaven.

Here's the analogy: pretend for a second the livelihood of your family depends on how many people you lead to Jesus. Again, we do not get benefits from this, but pretend for a second it was your entire livelihood. How would this fact change the way you approach people who have yet to meet Jesus? How much time would you spend with people who have yet to meet Jesus? Would they be your friends? Would you be kinder? Would you lay awake at night praying for them and begging God to help you know what to say, how to say it, and when to say whatever you are supposed to say the next time you are with them? Would you bash the things they believe and trash the people they look up to? Wouldn't you be very careful not to polarize the relationship or burn the bridge? Remember, your livelihood is on the line here.

Okay, your livelihood is not on the line, but their soul is. Which is more important?

We have to stop forcing our way. We must trust the Lordship of Christ, and the power of the Holy Spirit. All we are is His ambassadors of reconciliation. We reconcile people who have no knowledge of God, as well as those who vehemently oppose Him. We are not superior to anyone, nor do we have authority to demand our way. Jesus taught us to serve, not be served, in every aspect of life. We are called to build relationships and reconcile the entire world to the Father. The Holy Spirit will convict them; we need not try. We can be their friends just like Jesus was.

What do we do with government?

Jesus is the King of kings and The Lord of lords. We have no reason for panic. We can be at peace knowing He is still firmly on the throne and everything that is happening is under His control.

Romans 13:1-2 "Let everyone be subject to the governing authorities, for there is no authority except that which God has established. The authorities that exist have been established by God. Consequently, whoever rebels against the authority is rebelling against what God has instituted, and those who do so will bring judgment on themselves." (NIV)

Proverbs 21:1-2 "In the LORD's hand the king's heart is a stream of water that he channels toward all who please him. A person may think their own ways are right, but the LORD weighs the heart." (NIV)

We have nothing to fear. In fact, we should fear God and no one else. God will channel the hearts of leadership in the way He wants them to go. We should share the love of Jesus with all people and we should vote. As people find Jesus they will be guided by the Holy Spirit to vote as He leads them. God really does have the whole world under his control, including our country.

If God is calling you to get involved in politics, you should go for it. We need people with Godly integrity in office. Outside these options, we must trust God has the best interest of every person in the world. God is looking out for us, our children, grandchildren, great grandchildren, and beyond. God is on the throne.

Prayer is far more powerful than slander

> *1 Timothy 2:1-4 "I urge, then, first of all, that petitions, prayers, intercession and thanksgiving be made for all people—for kings and all those in authority, that we may live peaceful and quiet lives in all godliness and holiness. This is good, and pleases God our Savior, who wants all people to be saved and to come to knowledge of the truth." (NIV)*

We should fervently pray for our leaders and for the salvation of all people. Participating in gossip, perpetuating slander, and being politically charged is nothing more than throwing rocks at mankind. God has given us the amazing privilege of prayer.

When we pray, God does act on our behalf, as well as change our hearts where we need it.

What do we do with people who are not in the church?

We are commanded to be reconcilers of mankind. Sharing the love of Jesus is done through love, honesty, grace, and compassion; not anger, hatred, slander, and judgment. We should be kind to all people regardless of their moral, ethical, spiritual, or political beliefs. Some Christians choose to bash other Christians who take this approach. Jesus was known as *a friend of sinners* and if we are following Him, we will be also.

We build friendships because God loves all people and He **_commands_** us to do the same. We should share Jesus with all people and as they find Him, their hearts will be changed from the inside out. As their hearts change, they will support and vote for leadership that honors God. Leadership will change when people love God and elect those who will serve and please Him.

How can we get along with each other?

Fear has motivated the Church to segregate itself from society and become a subculture that neither understands nor relates to the world we abandoned. We have become paralyzed by fear. This paranoia has even caused us to turn on each other. Thousands of Christians have been gossiped about, shamed, and attacked by people who call themselves brothers and sisters in Christ. People have left the Church in droves and many still are barely surviving. Jesus said in John 10:10, *"The thief's (the Devil's) purpose is to steal and kill and destroy. My (Jesus') purpose is to give them a rich and satisfying life." (NLT) (clarification added)*

Millions of people have gone to church only to be saddled with shame, guilt, and coercion. Every part of their lives has been manipulated and controlled: how they dress, talk, walk, and act, what they listen to, what they read, who their friends are, how often they pray or read scripture, who they vote for, where they go on vacation, and on and on. Instead of their lives getting better they are saddled with more weight upon shoulders.

The Church has tirelessly labored to declare what we are against. Our fear has made us come across as desperate and angry. We seem to have forgotten what we are for, and what we are supposed to do. The fascination with what not to do, rather than what to do, has resulted in many churches not seeing any new people come to Christ for years, if not decades.

Jesus said in John 13:35 "Your love for one another will prove to the world that you are my disciples." (NLT) Fighting with each other over beliefs and behaviors is just the beginning of our internal struggle. People leave churches everyday because they no longer feel the way they once felt. They don't feel fed! Christians all over America have forgotten they are supposed to be feeding others; they are supposed to be fishing for men. Instead, they attend church purely for consumption. If they can't get the same feeling of satisfaction week after week, they simply go to another "restaurant."

In reality, we never stay the same; we either grow or atrophy. This is true as individuals and organizations. The grave mistake we make is when we complain about changes, attack leadership, and solicit support from others to confirm our internal anxiety. We may or may not intend to, but the result of such behavior is the forming of political factions that enact force to further our personal agenda.

Fighting over personal preferences is all about control, power, and selfishness. Demanding our way and throwing a fit to get things the way we prefer is all about self and does nothing but tear the Church apart and destroy our witness for Jesus. Jesus called us to take up our cross and follow Him daily. He modeled what it meant to lay down His life, asking us if we are willing to be living sacrifices for Him.

Stop fighting for your preferences and start serving. Be one of the people who put the food in the trough, not an overweight heifer that needs to go to slaughter. You will be amazed at how your faith will come alive if you move back into the world, make some friends who are not followers of Jesus, and invite them to the church where you love your fellow brothers and sisters in Christ and generously give your life away.

I close with these questions: can we be servants of God and trust He has all things under control? Can we stop blaming the government for the sin in our country and take responsibility for our failure to reach our nation? Can we serve all people and bring the love, forgiveness, and reconciliation of Jesus to them? Can we love each other and not have to control what others say or do? Can we ask how we can help, rather than demand how we want to be served? I know we can. It is not hopeless! It is not that the engine is blown and the Church needs a complete rebuild, we just have some critical parts needing adjustments. We can change this. The question is, will we?

I am sorry for the hatred that has been spread through gossip and slander in the political arena. I am sorry for the political factions within the church. And I am especially sorry for the many people who have been caught in the crosshairs and or crossfire of church politics. Please forgive us?

Questions:

1. Do you have fear about what is going to happen to our country?
2. Does your fear keep you up at night?
3. Have you slandered governmental parties or candidates you disagree with?
4. Have you immersed yourself in political propaganda and fear?
5. Have you blamed the government for the sin in our country?
6. Do you surround yourself with only people who believe what you believe?
7. Do you have any personal friendships with people who do not share your faith or political views?
8. Have you ever gossiped about or slandered people in your church or church leadership?
9. Have you tried to control what others believe or do?
10. Do you complain about different preferences you have in your church, i.e. music, sound, preaching style, different colors, pews vs. chairs, pastor's style of dress,

or any other non-biblical absolute?

11. Do you talk to your friends about your feelings and opinions of what is going wrong?

12. Do you owe family, friends, neighbors, or people in your community an apology?

13. Do you owe your church leadership or fellow members an apology?

Chapter 6: Angry

Ephesians 4:26-27 "And 'don't sin by letting anger control you.' Don't let the sun go down while you are still angry, for anger gives a foothold to the devil." (NLT)

In the year between my mom and my dad coming to Christ, I had the choice of attending church or staying home with Dad and watching football. With a choice like that, at eleven years old, I usually chose staying home with Dad. After Dad gave his life to Christ, there was only one choice. The whole Morgan clan went to church no matter what. This change was like taking my brother and I and moving us to China. We didn't understand the culture or the customs. We had no idea what they were talking about, and we hadn't a clue how to behave. To say the least, we were an absolute handful. Every week we got in trouble for something we did or said.

Most of the adults had no idea what to do with us. Every time we walked through the doors it seemed they were always angry about something. If Adolf Hitler and the Church Lady hooked-up and had a son, he would have been slightly nicer than my brother's Sunday school teacher. Every week my little bro complained about going to church until finally one Sunday he broke down in tears of refusal. Come to find out his teacher's way of making him behave was forcing him to put his nose in the corner for twenty minutes while the other kids did the fun part of the lesson. Nothing like winning kids with the anger of Jesus, right? I was a bit older and somehow understood I was just as intimidating to the teachers as they were to me, so I would say outrageous things just to push their buttons. This made it somewhat amusing, but being only twelve, I often crossed the line without knowing it.

The best part about church was the girls. In the seventh grade, my girlfriend was the most beautiful girl in church. She was a year older and all the guys including the upperclassman wanted to date her. We always sat together in the youth row, secretly holding hands, passing notes, and making fun of the older people during the service. One Sunday after the sermon, as we got up to leave, I gave her a little pinch on the backside, or as Forrest Gump would say, "The buttocks". What I didn't realize was the pastor's wife was sitting directly behind us, just inches away from the infraction. Yes, she saw the whole thing. After sitting through the entire sermon watching us giggling and passing notes, she was ready to come unglued. She was usually very nice to me, but week after week of fielding the volunteer's complaints of my behavior, coupled with the inappropriate touch, was the straw that broke the camel's back. She didn't say anything directly to me. She just gave me a look like…well you can imagine the kind of look that says, "You're about to lose your tiny, little, pathetic, bottom-grabbing life." I didn't have anything witty or intelligent to say, so I simply stood there stunned. She made a beeline for my mom, so I just avoided the issue, knowing I was totally busted. My backside still hurts from that event.

Ever since I became a pastor, one of my hot buttons is over hyper disciplinary tactics by church people. Growing up, my perception of adults in church was they were totally ticked off and hated being there just as much as I did. Looking back now, I realize it was a small group of control freaks that ruined it for the masses. Truth is, I deserved all the discipline I could get, but I was just a kid, a foreigner in an unknown land. I had no idea how to fit in with "those people." If it weren't for a small handful of adults who genuinely cared, I think I would be a casualty of church like so many others I grew up with.

Those few adults who chose to invest in me are my heroes; they showed me the love of Jesus and made becoming a Christian appealing. (The pastor's wife included) When I was completely unlovable, they accepted me and became my friend before I deserved it.

In this chapter, we are going to talk about anger. Far too many people think of the Church as a giant sea of angry people crashing into each other. Most of the friends I grew up with in church feel they barely escaped, and they won't go back for anything. The last thing they want is to subject their kids to what they went through.

Anger – A Very Complicated Emotion

When it comes to anger, it's almost never about one single person or event. Anger builds, festers, and stews deep inside us, surfacing itself in all kinds of emotional weather. When people come into our churches they are bringing a past with many stories just as we do. The difference is they are new and they don't know anything about us except, as professing Christians, we are supposed to be like Jesus. I'm extremely sensitive when it comes to working with kids because they have built-in human emotional radar. Adults can also sense these emotions but our radar has constant interference from the complications of life. Even when emotions are carefully hidden away, people "especially kids" can read us like a cheap novel.

The first thing we must understand about anger is anger is an *emotion* not a *sin*. We feel emotions all the time: happy, sad, energetic, fatigued, carefree, tense, turned-on, turned-off, etc. Anger is an emotion that all people feel. In fact, it gives me incredible comfort to know Jesus not only got angry, He let his emotions show.

John 2:13-17 "It was nearly time for the Jewish Passover celebration, so Jesus went to Jerusalem. In the Temple area he saw merchants selling cattle, sheep, and doves for sacrifices; he also saw dealers at tables exchanging foreign money. Jesus made a whip from some ropes and chased them all out of the Temple. He drove out the sheep and cattle, scattered the moneychangers' coins over the floor, and turned over their tables. Then, going over to the people who sold doves, he told them, 'Get these things out of here. Stop turning my Father's house into a marketplace!' Then his disciples remembered this prophecy from the Scriptures: 'Passion for God's house will consume me.'"(NLT)

Passion for God's house consumed Him. Jesus had a tremendous amount of passion displayed in all kinds of ways. On this occasion, one of those ways was through the emotion of anger. Being angry is not sinful and having passion is not wrong. To be a true follower of Jesus you will have to have some grit, because following Christ is not easy.

In our society today, anger is one of the few acceptable emotions we are permitted to let out. Admitting we are hurt reveals weakness, being frustrated shows a lack of decisiveness, remaining too calm appears passive, and getting really excited seems immature. It sometimes feels like our only two options are contained happiness or anger. Many Christians today mistake anger for passion. Anger does not prove passion any more than physical contact proves love.

It seems some Christians excuse constant anger as passion, giving themselves permission to act out their anger whenever and however they want. They're mad about abortion, immorality, homosexuality, the public school system, what is happening at church, work, the community, and in their own homes. They're ticked and they want everyone to know it. The problem is continual anger is impossible to be around. This is why many people turn and run every time they see a Christian. Yes, Jesus got angry at the religious leaders extorting money from people who were trying to genuinely worship, but Jesus was not angry all the time and Jesus did not sin in His anger.

Anger is not sinful in and of itself. Jesus never sinned, but as we have seen, He did get angry. The difficulty in anger is controlling our emotions, not allowing them to take control of us. The temptation is to say or do hurtful things that we wish we could take back later. Anger is not a sin, but it is extremely easy to sin while being angry.

It is wise to note in the Gospels of Matthew and Mark that this incident is directly followed by the chief priests and the teachers feeling so threatened they began to plan how to crucify Jesus. Anger can and will provoke equal or greater reaction from those we display our anger towards.

Where does our anger come from?

Anger can be induced by relationships or events that happen around us. It is extremely easy to allow all negative emotions to turn into anger. For example, many Christians become overwhelmed when talking with a friend or enemy who has differing beliefs. For example; a friend makes a very compelling, educated, and logical argument against our faith that we can't immediately refute. After further debate we run out of ammunition and have no idea what to say next. Instead of recognizing their position, admitting they have excellent points and politely asking for time to look into the subject deeper, we get angry and threaten them with eternal damnation. We allow our lack of knowledge to frustrate us because we feel threatened.

Another example is the fear we have with our children being influenced by immorality. Instead of expressing our fear appropriately we get angry and yell. Instead of being involved in the school system, PTA, or community organizations, we fight or boycott them in anger. Fear is anger's kissing cousin. Admitting fear often feels like weakness. Rather than working for positive change and genuine solutions we throw up our hands in disgust, take our toys, and leave.

The feeling of moral superiority is yet another. Because we embrace Scripture as absolute truth, we arrogantly flaunt Biblical values and try desperately to force our morals on the rest of society. Far too many Christians slam their fists on the counter, stomp their feet, raise their voices, and slander people who don't hold the same beliefs they have. When we are confused, hurt, embarrassed, tired, flustered, or lack knowledge, we find ourselves not knowing what to say so we simply explode. Because we don't know how to discern our emotions and lack the ability to communicate in more positive and effective ways, we lash out in anger. This may shut the other person down in the moment but the lasting impact is something we will not prefer.

Do you ever just wake up on the wrong side of the bed feeling angry? Anger can be internally induced by multiple trigger points. I have no idea why, but sometimes I just feel ticked-off. Before I gave my life to Christ, I had some real anger management issues. After giving my life to Christ, it has been a long, hard struggle to recognize my feelings and deal with them. Sometimes I just get in a funk. Tina didn't do anything; the kids are great, nothing bad happened at work, things are cool with the neighbors, and my friendships are solid. But for no legitimate reason I am totally agitated and angry. I hate to admit this but in some ways it is just my personality. I lean towards confrontation so when people start talking about what ticks them off I find myself getting angry, too.

Tina and I have been married for 22 years; we met in high school and have been through a ton of stuff together. I can honestly say, I passionately love her and she loves me, too. With that said, we sometimes get on each other's nerves. Yes, we get mad at each other. Sometimes our anger has nothing to do with the other. Sometimes we're angry and we have no idea why. In the last several years, we have been learning to detect where our anger is coming from. If it is directly related to each other, we have learned communication tools to help us work through our stuff without hurting each other or sinning. If our anger has nothing to do with the other person, we have learned to say, "I don't know why I am so ticked-off. It has nothing to do with you, but I am totally frustrated right now and could use some space." We are learning to give each other room to explore our true feelings, as well as, the time to express them.

There are many great communication tools. Recognizing our emotions is a good first step. Whether it is with each other, the neighbors, people at work, or our church family, we can't afford to just let it fly. We need to deal with our stuff by tapping into the help of the Holy Spirit, trusted friends, and even professional counselors when needed. Marriages are crumbling, churches are splitting, and people are running away from Christianity because we can't control and or communicate how we feel.

How does this play out in church?

Above, I gave a very small snapshot of life in the Morgan home. We have been in ministry for the past twenty-two years and there have been countless Sundays that our life is not going perfect, yet week after week we go to church and try to minister to other people. I bet you have gone to church, possibly even fulfilled your role as a staff member or volunteer while you were really angry or upset. There are many things all of us deal with every day. The truth is, we are never dealing with just one thing at a time. God calls all His followers to help each other grow spiritually by faithfully serving in the Church--growing together in healthy relationships while we work through our individual stuff. It's hard enough to represent ourselves well, let alone all that Jesus is in the process.

Think about it: even getting ready for church, out the door and down the road can be an extremely upsetting process. We wake up agitated, the kids are in full bloom being kids, our spouse says something off tilt, the usual person is late while the usual early person complains, we argue all the way to church, get out of the car, smile and wave at friends as we walk across the parking lot, shake the greeter's hand, pretend everything is perfect, drop off the kids in their classes, and go to the places we volunteer. As people come into our class, Bible study, or small group, they bring their pile of stuff with them too. Church is where lives crash directly into each other like emotional bumper cars.

We come together carrying our stack of emotions with

underlying preconceived idea that the only acceptable emotions to express are happiness and anger. I don't know why, but most people I talk to feel the Church wants everyone to be fine. "We are all doing fine, life is going great, and we are all totally victorious over sin. Amen and Hallelujah! (Puke)"... It seems like the Church wants everyone to be perfect instead of healthy, whole, authentic followers of Christ. We seem to be producing hypocrites who wish they could be real. It's to the point where most people have no idea how to be honest, let alone deal with what is truly going on in their lives.

Many Christians are walking time bombs, ticking away as they rub shoulders up and down the halls of the church. Because they feel a tremendous pressure to be perfect, they bottle it all up until the pressure becomes so great they explode. If we become too jaded, we simply stop trying to be perfect, let our true anger show and become known as the Christian grump that everyone tries to avoid. Its no wonder people feel so out of place in church.

Emotional Road Signs

If you have given your life to Christ, the Bible says you have the Holy Spirit living inside you. The Bible teaches the Holy Spirit produces a fruit that grows out of our lives as He lives in us. This fruit is called the fruit of the spirit. This "one" amazing fruit has the most incredible nutrients; love, joy, peace, patience, kindness, goodness, gentleness, faithfulness, and self-control. (Galatians 5:22-23 NIV) In the Biblical time period, it was an agricultural society, so to them this analogy was abundantly clear. As a Christ Follower these are the things that grow out of the soil of your life. Being a much more mobile society, we might use transportation as an example. For instance, as we travel down the road of life, going the same direction as Jesus, "following Him," the road signs should continually read love, joy, peace, patience, kindness, goodness, gentleness, faithfulness, and self-control. Meaning, we will feel, act, and relate to others with love, joy, peace, patience, kindness, goodness, gentleness, faithfulness, and self-control.

We live in the Seattle area. When we get on the main freeway, I-5, we are either heading north or south. As soon as you get on the freeway, you see signs that say north or south, Portland or Vancouver. We scoot down the freeway with complete confidence because the road signs continually remind us of our direction. As Christians traveling down the road of life, we should continuously see love, joy, peace, patience, kindness, goodness, gentleness, faithfulness, and self-control, as the road signs indicating our direction. If we continually see un-forgiveness, anger, rage, unfaithfulness, impatience, unhappiness, frustration, evil, and agitation, we might want to slow down, stop, and seriously evaluate which direction we are headed.

Again, being angry is not sinful; it is an emotion everyone feels, including Jesus. Anger can be a very dangerous emotion though. Think about it. With this one emotion, we can wipe out all the nutrients in the fruit of the Spirit.

Controlling our anger and knowing when and how to appropriately express it is extremely difficult. Before we go deeper in this chapter, I want to encourage you. If you feel angry a lot, ask God to take you on a journey of self-discovery to will help you unpack why. It is worth doing whatever it takes. Your marriage, family, and witness for Christ all depend on it.

Biblical Guidelines for Anger

Jesus lived a sinless life. In His sinless life, He displayed the emotion of anger. This is very encouraging, because we know it is totally possible to be angry and not sin. When we were first married, our arguments often turned into anger and many times we found ourselves saying things we had to apologize for; both to each other and to God. My apologies often were led by, "I know I shouldn't have said that, but I was so angry." I wish it were not true, but I have said that line to my wife, family members, friends, people in the Church, neighbors, and even complete strangers.

Have you ever done something in anger and wished you could take it back? Have you ever felt out of control while you were angry? Have you ever said things that were untrue, hurtful, and blatantly mean while you were angry? If you answered yes to any of those questions, you and I are a lot alike. The people in Ephesus are a lot like us too.

Ephesians 4:21-32 "Since you have heard about Jesus and

have learned the truth that comes from him, throw off your old sinful nature and your former way of life, which is corrupted by lust and deception. Instead, let the Spirit renew your thoughts and attitudes. Put on your new nature, created to be like God—truly righteous and holy. So stop telling lies. Let us tell our neighbors the truth, for we are all parts of the same body. ***And 'don't sin by letting anger control you.' Don't let the sun go down while you are still angry, for anger gives a foothold to the devil.*** *If you are a thief, quit stealing. Instead, use your hands for good hard work, and then give generously to others in need.* ***Don't use foul or abusive language. Let everything you say be good and helpful, so that your words will be an encouragement to those who hear them. And do not bring sorrow to God's Holy Spirit by the way you live.*** *Remember, he has identified you as his own, guaranteeing that you will be saved on the day of redemption.* ***Get rid of all bitterness, rage, anger, harsh words, and slander, as well as all types of evil behavior. Instead, be kind to each other, tenderhearted, forgiving one another, just as God through Christ has forgiven you.*** *(NLT) (Bold/underline emphasis added)*

This passage of Scripture is not saying it is sinful to be angry. However it is crystal clear that anger is a very difficult thing to control. In fact, we are instructed not to stay angry overnight because anger gives the devil a foothold in our lives. Anger makes us want to use foul language, become loud and even violent. Anger festers in un-forgiveness and turns into hate. Have you ever been around someone, or you yourself, been angry towards a person or a group of people for an extended period of time? Being around people who are bitter, angry, and full of hate darkens even the brightest days. Even if they aren't mad at you. Anger literally rots the soul from the inside out and repels all others not sharing the same sentiment.

I feel so bad for people who allow anger to control their life. It seems everything they see, do, and talk about revolves around anger. We not only sin in our anger, saying and doing things we shouldn't, we become sour and miserable on the inside. The frightening reality of anger is that it is an incredible source of fuel. Did you ever notice how anger can keep you up late into the night and then turn right around and wake you early the next morning? Anger can keep a person motivated for years. Many people have become very successful out of spite. Tragically, even in the light of success, the deep dark hole of anger locks its victims in a prison of self-misery.

The Bible says, "The joy of the Lord is our strength." Anger is the polar opposite of joy. It consumes joy, giving the elusion of strength while rotting us from the inside out. If we allow ourselves to remain angry, we become so sour no one can stand being around us. Millions of senior citizens sit alone in their retirement centers, angry that no one wants to spend time with them. Thousands of churches are dying slow deaths all over the country, wondering why last week's guests never come back. I can't think of a better example of *John 10:10, "The thief's purpose is to kill rob and destroy, but I have come to give you a rich and satisfying life." (NLT – Jesus Christ)*

Anger can ruin relationships, steal your joy, and rob your peace, while keeping you alive to live another day, month, year, or decade in utter isolation. It's nothing short of emotional crucifixion.

Sadly, many Christians are all shriveled up inside from anger, bitterness and un-forgiveness. Many Christians have been so polarizing to the people in their community that they have no one left to fight with except each other. I am convinced this is one of the biggest reasons why so many church people fight over music, color of carpet, dress codes and any other crazy thing they can point their angry finger at. These emotions churn in the soul of our heart like a giant twister sweeping away love, joy, peace, patience, kindness, goodness, gentleness, faithfulness and self-control. This tragedy not only destroys the abundant life God has for us, it destroys our witness for Christ. Much of society views Christians as angry killjoys who suck the fun out of life.

What are we so mad about?

It's impossible to reconcile relationships through anger. This is important to remember because Jesus gave every Christian the ministry of reconciling the world to God. Sadly, one of our greatest downfalls in the Church is righteous indignation. We become intolerant and indignant toward people because they do the very things God set us free from.

Allow me to explain by using an example of my personal self-righteous indignation. Both of my parents grew up in alcoholic homes. It was a family heritage tracing as far back in our family tree as we can see. My dad started smoking and drinking in elementary school. By the time us kids were born he smoked two packs of cigarettes a day and had a very strong addiction to alcohol. Now I want to be clear, I don't think smoking is a sin. It is a very bad health choice but I cannot say it is a biblical absolute no more than I can say eating donuts and bacon everyday is. Drinking alcohol is not sinful either. The Bible is very clear on the fact that Jesus drank wine, and Paul encouraged Timothy to have a little wine with his dinner to help his stomach.

However, drunkenness is a sin, so the way my dad drank was sinful. When he gave his life to Jesus he knew he needed to stop drinking all together. For Dad, one drink always led to another and another and another until he was drunk. Like many smokers he hated the expense and the constant need to have a cigarette. In addition Mom hated the smell, so Dad wanted to stop drinking and smoking completely.

Every day he pleaded with God to miraculously take away his addictions. One day he felt God saying to him, "I'll take them if you will give them to me." Instantly, he knew what that meant. He had just purchased a new carton of cigarettes and had gallons of alcohol in the cupboards. First he said a prayer with my mom, then he threw the new carton of cigarettes in the wood stove, went straight upstairs and emptied the cupboards, dumping all the alcohol down the drain. He will tell you that he has never had a withdrawal or craving since and I have never seen my dad smoke or drink again. God did a miracle for my dad and our family. I wish it happened that way for all people but for most it is a process they have to truly fight for.

This was huge for our family. For years we'd had to ride in an oxygen deprived blue cloud of smoke as our family drove down the road. For years we'd had to have that horrible smell and mess in our house. Dad was a lot of fun when he was drunk and was never abusive, but having him sober on the weekends did make our family time far better. This was a very positive life change for us. Because both sides of our family have a long line of alcoholics and drug addicts, we all have very passionate feelings about these issues. My mom and Dad broke the alcoholic cycle in our family, and now none of their kids drink and only one of their grandkids smokes and drinks alcohol. This is a huge deal for our family.

Can I confess something to you? For the longest time, especially as a young Christian, I looked at people who smoked and drank with eyes of disgust and anger. It was not that I meant to, but God had taken that out of our family. Cigarettes, drugs and alcohol represent extremely destructive things in my world. Every time I see someone smoking I can't help but picture some poor little kid trapped inside a car where they can hardly breathe. Every time I got around alcohol, all I could picture was people in a drunken stupor. Just the smell of alcohol flooded my heart with emotions I was not prepared for. I hate to admit it but in the past I have been vocally judgmental and angry towards people over these issues.

God has done an amazing work in me in this area. When I say work, I mean I have had to change. With his help I must admit I am still in process. I used to try and hide these feelings, but anger and disgust are not things you can conceal. People could sense my emotions by the way I looked at them, postured myself and carried on conversations. People can tell when we are disgusted, angry or upset. This deeply affects our friendships with them and can even ruin our witness. My anger towards the destruction our family has experienced was, and still is, sometimes projected onto others. I was angry and viewed cigarettes and alcohol as the source of my anger, rather than a destructive addiction people can become trapped in.

Who should we be mad at?

We've all experienced the prison of sin. If through finding Jesus we have escaped some of them, we never want to go back again. The slightest glimpse of those issues produces reactions we are not often prepared for. In some ways it's like being saved from drowning. Because we were drowning in water – water not being good or evil... The drowning experience can produce such a fear of water we never go swimming again. Just as there are many factors and variables to sin there are many factors and variables to drowning. The problem is, God has called us to be *rescue swimmers*, to seek and to save those that are lost. When we project our fears, anger, and frustration at specific issues, people take it as a personal attack on them. The issues are not the problem nor are the people. Our struggle is neither against behaviors nor the people whom carry them out.

*Ephesians 6:10-17 "A final word: Be strong in the Lord and in his mighty power. Put on all of God's armor so that you will be able to stand firm against all strategies of the devil. **<u>For we are not fighting against flesh-and-blood enemies, but against evil rulers and authorities of the unseen world, against mighty powers in this dark world, and against evil spirits in the heavenly places.</u>** Therefore, put on every piece of God's armor so you will be able to resist the enemy in the time of evil. Then after the battle you will still be standing firm. Stand your ground, putting on the belt of truth and the body armor of God's righteousness. For shoes, put on the peace that comes from the Good News so that you will be fully prepared. In addition to all of these, hold up the shield of faith to stop the fiery arrows of the devil. Put on salvation as your helmet, and take the sword of the Spirit, which is the word of God."*

(NLT)(Emphasis added)

Sin is unbelievably destructive. Once you have been set free from things that have brought pain in your life, it's only natural to be angry at those behaviors and people who do them. But, our passion has an alignment problem. As people who follow The Living God, who have the power of the Holy Spirit living in us, we must be aware of the spiritual battle that is happening around us. Our focus should be on the one who brings sin, tempts with sin, and ruins people by holding them captive to it. Our focus need not be on the sins or on those who do them. There is something much deeper happening in the spiritual realm. I have always thought of the armor of God as protection, but as I have studied that passage more intently it seems the armor is much more offensive in nature. We are supposed to be fighting the devil on behalf of people.

This is extremely difficult because sin is not only destructive to those doing the sinning; it also deeply affects all people connected to them. Sin can even have enormous consequences on innocent bystanders. Directing anger towards people gives our emotions a place to land and can even make us feel like we are righteously sticking up for God, but people are not the root of the problem.

About nine years ago we became aware of a family member having an affair. We watched the pain this was creating in our relative and anticipated the pain that was coming for their kids. To be totally transparent, I wanted to rip him apart. The first affair she forgave and we as a family had to walk through the forgiveness and restoration process with her. I can't tell you how hard it was for me to even sit in the same room with him let alone talk with him like *a friend*. The only thing I could lean on was that God loves him and wants desperately to reconcile the broken relationship between Him and His son. This relative was not just missing the mark for his marriage; he was missing the mark of God's standards. Me ripping him apart would only make the situation worse.

Before he went off the reservation we were fairly close; he was my brother-in-law but I considered him a trusted friend. After the first affair our relationship was never the same. We no longer shared the same value system or belief in God. For the next few years it was like walking on eggshells every time we were together. We sensed there was more going on and as time marched on our dark suspicions were validated. He had some very serious sexual addictions and his unfaithfulness continued to grow. She chose to divorce him because he couldn't be trusted.

Even through the divorce we had to choose to forgive him and continue to be kind. We couldn't afford to let our emotions and selfish desires get the best of us. God has called us to be reconcilers not defensemen.

I can't begin to tell you how hard it is to pray good things for him, but we do. We don't see him much anymore but when we do it is so hard to be kind to him, but we are. There is something at stake here that goes far deeper and lasts much longer than this lifetime. His eternity is at stake; not only that, his kids need a Godly dad. He has had two other children with a girlfriend and those kids need a godly dad too. He knows what he has done is absolutely wrong and he knows he is far from God. In fact, he actually said to me he doesn't even know if he believes in God anymore. He doubts if he ever did. It's amazing how we live in a world that actually thinks if they don't believe in something than it is not real.

There are some very certain realities we believe in as Christ- followers. The first is that God loves all people and he longs to have a personal relationship with them. The second is Jesus gives us access to the Father through the forgiveness of our sins that He paid for on the cross. The third is without making Jesus the leader and Lord of your life, no one will make it into Heaven. This is extremely real and this is something we could not be more serious about. If we harbor un-forgiveness towards people, get angry, and shun them, they could be lost for all eternity. If we are not very careful, we could be the biggest roadblock people face in finding a true relationship with the Living God.

Please understand, forgiveness, love, and trust are all very different things. We love and forgive our ex-brother-in-law but we do not trust him at all. We can be friendly to him, pray for God's best in his life, and encourage him to give his life back to Christ.

We are not fighting him; we are fighting Satan. The devil is trying to kill rob and destroy everything in his life and up to this point he has succeeded in many ways. We are going to fight for his kids and for his soul, because God has called us to reconcile him through the forgiveness of Christ. This does not make us superior to him or anyone else; it just makes us obedient to God. Look at what Jesus said to His disciples when He sent them out to talk with the public.

Matthew 10:16 "Look, I am sending you out as sheep among wolves. So be as shrewd as snakes and harmless as doves."
(NLT)

The anger we have towards sin is often misdirected at people who are committing sins. When our anger points toward them, all they feel is hatred. This provokes them to fight. Their wrath exponentially grows with every rude, disrespectful, arrogant, condescending, threatening, and angry word that

comes out of our mouths. Remember what happened after Jesus turned over the tables and chased the moneychangers out of the temple? They plotted his execution. Jesus didn't even sin in his anger; he did not judge their spiritual condition, swear at them, beat them or slander them. He just had passion for the house of God. In His anger Jesus stayed between the lines while He brought correction.

For many Christians anger doesn't just last a couple of nights. Many Christians have stayed angry for months, years and even decades. For many Christians, anger is defining their entire life. The reason we are loosing the battle is because we are fighting on the wrong battlefield. **The fight we are engaged in is not against people and the issues are not the battlefield.** *People* **are whom we are fighting for, and the battlefield is in the spiritual realm, against a spiritual foe.**

We must stop being angry with people and start fighting with love.

The disciple Peter wrote, *"Love covers over a multitude of sins." (NIV)* 1 Peter 4:8 Peter was the disciple who was the burly fisherman. He was most likely the guy who grabbed his sword and cut off the guard's ear when they came to arrest Jesus. Peter was the guy who was always ready for a fight. He was the one who told Jesus he would die for him; they would never take him alive. Peter, Mr. Tough Guy, writes, "Love covers over a multitude of sins." Did Peter get soft? Did Peter become one of those sissy Christians? No! Peter had a front

row, center stage seat, to the life of Jesus. Peter was there,
Peter watched his Lord and Savior willingly go to the cross to
save all people; he watched Jesus forgive the very people who
were crucifying Him as they were in the act of doing it. Peter
discovered what Jesus meant when he talked about the meek
inheriting the earth.

Being meek does not mean you are weak; being meek
shows unbelievable strength under control. Jesus had all the
power and strength in the universe. Jesus could have called
down fire from Heaven killing all that were mocking Him,
beating Him, and nailing Him to the cross. But Jesus kept His
strength under control. The Bible says while Jesus was in the
grave he went into Hades and took the keys to death from the
devil. The Bible says, because of His awesome sacrifice, God
gave Jesus the name that is above all names. The Bible says
that Jesus won and He will be the judge at the end of the age.
Jesus beat the devil with... Love.

As Peter wrote those words I can totally see him
remembering all the time he spent with Jesus. Remember when
the religious leaders brought the woman caught in adultery to
Jesus? Those peeping Toms caught a woman in the act of
adultery. The law clearly states if a person is caught in the act
of adultery they must be stoned to death. The religious leaders
caught this lady in the act and drug her before Jesus. Interesting
that they didn't bring the man. But they did bring her. They
went before Jesus with rocks in hand, ready to execute the law.
They testified against her and asked Jesus to judge her. Jesus
bent down to the ground, wrote something in the dirt and then

stood up. He said, "You who have no sin? Throw the first stone."

The older guys knew right away - The trick was up, and quickly they dropped their stones and walked away in disgust. The younger guys took a little longer but finally, one by one, they threw down their rocks and stomped away. Jesus looked the woman in the eyes. This woman who had betrayed her husband, betrayed the man's wife, betrayed her family, and betrayed God. He looked straight into her eyes with deep love and compassion and said, "Woman, where are your accusers?" I'm sure she could barely look up, but as she did, probably for the first time in her life, her eyes caught a glimpse of true love, complete acceptance, and total forgiveness. He said, "You have no accusers, neither do I accuse you. Go and sin no more." Peter witnessed this with his own eyes. The most incredibly powerful leader in the universe withheld his power for wrath, and in its place extended total forgiveness. He not only forgave her, he defended and protected her. Peter watched as love, compassion, forgiveness and meekness took over and changed a person's life forever.

If we truly want to represent Jesus to this world we must become more tolerant of people, while absolutely not tolerating the devil. Notice I didn't say, hate the sin but love the sinner. We have confused that statement and in some ways it has become the root of the problem. The devil is the origin of sin. For this reason we must turn our anger towards him not a certain sin. We must defeat him the same way Jesus did. "There is no greater love than this, that a man would lay down his life for his friends." Jesus said, "To follow Him, we must deny ourselves and take up our cross and follow him daily." Our cross includes being kind to a brother-in-law who betrays our sister, niece, and nephew. Our cross looks like people who serve rather than be served. Our cross looks like strength under control, not anger out of control.

Tolerance is not a word some Christians like to use because they feel like tolerance allows sin. Being tolerant of the devil I would agree is wrong. Being tolerant of people, showing them love and kindness in the middle of their mess is following the example of Jesus. Hating the devil and loving people is fighting the spiritual battle on the spiritual battlefield. Imagine what would happen if we spent the same amount of time praying for people as we do gossiping about them? Especially if we don't gossip about them before we pray! Imagine what would happen if we spent the same amount of time reaching out and serving people as we do slandering them? Imagine what would happen if we turned the anger we have towards sin against the one who steals robs and destroys?

Love is what conquers sin. I am so grateful to the men and women who chose to love me while I was at my worst. They are the ones that did battle for me. They are the ones that beat the devil while sparing me. Thank you so much. May we all follow your example and do likewise.

A Tribute to a Couple of My Heroes

In my opening story I mentioned if it were not for a handful of genuinely Christ-like people at the churches we attended, I would probably be just like the thousands who grew up attending church every Sunday but today refuse to step even one foot in the door. These few amazing adults loved me unconditionally and for that they are my heroes.

My first is Kim Hall. Kim was a lady who stood about six foot six and had a smile and laugh that would knock your socks off. She saw right through my boloney. I often said things just to get a rise out of my Sunday school teachers, but Kim never bit. She had a look that was unexplainable. In one sense you knew you crossed the line but in another you knew she genuinely liked you and was really glad you were there. One Sunday not long after the bottom-grabbing incident, my mom got a call after church. It was very normal for her to have someone talking to her after church about my brother's or my behavior, so she learned to leave as quickly as possible. Kim went looking for her after service but Mom had successfully dodged the bullet and made it home without incident. When Kim called I heard my sister say, "Mom, phone, it's Kim Hall from church." As soon as those words rang through the house I knew I was totally busted.

I quickly replayed our class in my mind, everything I said, everything she said, and everything my friends said. We did say a few things but it wasn't anything meriting a phone call. I thought to myself, "Maybe she has been holding back and storing things up for a few weeks." But nothing huge came to mind. I knew I was dead meat walking, but had no idea what for. That night my mom came to tuck me in bed and as she stood out in the hallway I could hear her crying. Now I knew I was dead. She came in wiping the tears from her eyes with a huge smile on her face. She said that she had been praying and asking God to show her my heart. She said that God had shown her my heart and it was much different than what I worked so hard at showing others. She said God had shown her that I deeply care about and love people. She said God told her I would be a pastor some day and that she loved me very much. Talk about weird! I thought I was going to get the whipping of a lifetime and she comes in with how great my heart is. The next day it got even weirder. My mom told me that I looked great and she was proud of me. What? Proud of me... Why?

When Kim called, she said, "Hello, Wanda, my name is Kim Hall, I am Matt's Sunday school teacher." Mom said, "Yes?" The silence became awkward so Kim continued, "I just wanted to call and tell you what a neat kid Matt is." My mom said, "I'm Wanda Morgan!" Kim said, "I know who you are and I know who Matt is. I wanted to call you today and encourage you. Matt is a tremendous handful and I have been praying and asking God to show me his heart. I have asked God to show me so I would have grace for him and be able to reach him where he is. God has shown me his heart and I figured that if I am having the struggles I am having in class, you are probably having the same type of struggles at home. I have a son too and I want you to know that I think Matt is a terrific kid and I want to encourage you to ask God to show you his heart."

My poor Mom was totally spent, she had no idea what to do with us, and here this lady was, the first person to call and not rag on her kids. This lady from church, a Sunday school teacher, called to encourage her and give her some very timely and crucial advice. This phone call not only changed my life, it probably saved it. Mom thanked Kim and before Kim hung up she said, "One more thing Wanda, one thing I have noticed about Matt is that he responds best to encouragement, so I also want to encourage you to find one thing good about Matt everyday and tell him several times what that is, even if it is he has beautiful eyes, tell him." In tears, Mom thanked her and hung up the phone.

I can't tell you how many times I have heard from my mom that I have beautiful eyes. See, I have baby blue eyes and God did a great job with them. I am very glad he did because there was many days when that was all mom could find good to say about me. She has become the greatest source of encouragement in my life. From that day on she started telling me how tender I was, how much I loved people and how I would one day be a pastor. My mom chose not to focus on what I wasn't, or on what I was. My mom chose to focus on what God made me to be and she sowed those things into my soul. Kim, my mom and God were right, and so were you. Thank you from the bottom of my heart.

As a side note: If you have challenging kids, anger is bound to come and go. My mom had many more angry moments with me after that day. With that said, can I say to you what Kim said to my mom? Kids respond better to encouragement. I have found our words can be prophetic when it comes to kids. They will become what we speak into them. If we tell them they are bad, stupid, inconsiderate, etc. that is exactly what they become. However if we sow into them what we see they can become, they will most likely become what we plant into the soil of their souls.

I have the richness of God and the awesome presence of the Holy Spirit in my life because a woman gave herself to prayer, the love of God, and his love for rebellious kids like me. There are many heroes on my journey. Brad and Phil, thank you so much. Dave, Gregg, Vicki, Mike and Kim, you guys saved my life, you are my heroes.

Did you know that if you are a Christ-follower, God has called you to be a hero to someone too? You can do it; you can be the hands, feet, arms, and legs of Christ to a world that desperately needs His love. They might not act like they want Jesus and they might not even believe Jesus is real, but through your friendship, kindness, love, and humility they will find Him?

Let's put the rocks down and start throwing our arms around a world that desperately needs love!

Questions:
1. What are the top five things that tick you off?
2. Who are the top five people who tick you off?
3. Would you be willing to take the time and pray about these things?
   a. Ask God to show you how to deal with the

issues that bother you.

    b. Ask God to show you the hearts of the people who have you so upset. Write down what He shares with you.

4. Is there someone you could call or go see and encourage?

    a. When are you going to do it?

5. Is there someone you need to apologize to for being angry with for longer than a day?

    a. When are you going to do it?

Chapter 7: Exclusive

1st John 4:18 *"There is no fear in love. But perfect love drives out fear, because fear has to do with punishment. The one who fears is not made perfect in love." (NIV)*

Have you ever wondered why the human race has to constantly be reminded not to segregate? Whether it is the cliques in school, those seemingly closed circles at church, or all out racism, people love to know where they fit. Why? One word… Fear! Fear drives us to be exclusive. "Us four and no more." "Tic tock the game is locked." We love our peeps and our peeps love us because we are afraid of how others might change things.

There is no word in the English language further from the heart and character of Jesus than *exclusive*. I looked up the etymology of the word and this is what I found: *"so as to exclude," Of monopolies, rights, franchises, of social circles, clubs, etc., "unwilling to admit outsiders," "keep out, shut out, hinder," ex- "out", "to close, shut", Exclude; excluding.*

When I first began in ministry I was a volunteer Youth Pastor at a small church. On our youth staff was a young man who just graduated from high school and was dating the pastor's daughter. Shortly after we began volunteering, this young man became riddled with guilt from things he should not be doing with his girlfriend. As the Holy Spirit convicted his heart, he went to the pastor, confessed what they were doing, and begged for forgiveness. Instead of forgiveness, he received a tongue-lashing that included expletives, threats, and expulsion. You can imagine the heartbreak; here he was trying to do the very thing pastors encourage people to do: repent from their sin and ask for forgiveness. In the place of forgiveness was a size eleven boot-print tattooed to his hindquarters. Punting him right out the door.

Completely beside himself, he came to me for advice. I tried to calm him by explaining he was dealing with a father first and "The Pastor" second. I attempted to excuse his rage and expletives by empathizing with his dad heart. I promised to go to the pastor and talk it through. When I went to the pastor, it was several days after the initial shock, so I was expecting remorse for the way he handled the situation and I looked forward to learning how to walk a person through the forgiveness process and earning back trust. I was completely caught off guard when the pastor not only stood behind what he said, he emphatically defended the need to exclude this young man and *anyone else who makes physical mistakes like this*.

I tried to understand the pastor's perspective, but as time marched on, I continued to see people being excluded for various things he feared. After that first year, the church offered to hire me on as their full-time Youth Pastor. In light of our philosophical differences, we could not in good conscience accept the position, so we graciously turned it down. Because we rejected the position, we received the same type of walking papers so many others had before us.

The next church I worked in was a much larger fellowship closer to the city. I shared my experience with some trusted friends on staff and they assured me that would never happen in their church. As the pastor of the junior high department, I had many kids under my care. Students are the most impressionable people in the world, so I understand parents need to protect their kids. Because of my background as an un-churched kid I have a passion for people who don't know Jesus. I see everything we do in the church as outreach. We constantly encouraged our students to bring their friends. Because of this, we saw many kids coming to church from all kinds of backgrounds. In short, the new kids didn't have a clue how to behave in church. They talked, walked, dressed, and acted like un-churched kids.

When parents, as well as, church leaders overheard kids swearing, or caught them smoking, they came unglued. They would not stand for kids wearing baggy jeans or hats in the church. It got worse! Some of the kids snuck off during youth services to smoke and do other creative things together. One of the teenage girls got pregnant. And as usual, some of the boys got into fights. Every time something "ungodly" happened a parent or a group of parents would complain to my boss about the "vile" behavior happening "at church" in front of their kids.

In anger, one parent said, "For Christ' sake!" I replied, "Exactly!" I meant we chose to love those kids for the sake of Christ, but they didn't get it. If the "bad" kids didn't change fast enough, the parents would literally run them off. When they weren't overtly asking them to leave, they went out of their way to shame them and threaten them with eternal damnation.

I served at that church for five years, desperately trying to reach lost kids; but every time we did, the church people ran them off because they were so afraid their kids would be infected by their bad influence. The straw that broke the camel's back was when the church refused to have a junior high drop-in program after school for latchkey kids. It was not the refusal that bothered me; it was the reason behind it. They didn't want to have "those kids" in "our building," because they would mess up the carpet, break things, and possibly steal valuables. It was clear to me they had no intention of accepting outsiders unless they were willing to convert to Christianity first and immediately conform to their behavioral standards.

I'm a father of three girls and I lead a church of my own now, so I understand the desire to protect our kids and facilities, but isn't it possible we have gone too far? Aren't we supposed to be reaching people who are far from God? If they are far from God, don't we expect they will act like and have habits that are typical for people who are far from Him? Don't we expect to deal with issues while we love them through the transformation the Bible clearly teaches the _Holy Spirit does_ from the inside out?

Are we a church or country club?

In Youth Ministry, exclusivity is one of the major issues a

leader deals with. The parents exclude kids who frighten them, and the kids exclude one another to climb the ladder of popularity. When I became a lead pastor of adults, I knew I would have to create a culture of acceptance and help parents not react to fear by excluding kids from our youth program. In Youth Ministry exclusivity is par for the course, but when I became a pastor of adults I thought the exclusivity issue would be left in the past. Boy was I wrong! Adults can be just as bad, if not worse. We are much more refined in the way we do, but I have learned exclusivity is prevalent in every age group.

We exclude people because they don't believe the same things we believe, act the way we think they should act, talk the way we think they should talk, or dress the way we think they should dress. In many ways the Church is like a country club. If you pay your dues, fulfill your pledge, stay within dress code, and don't rock the boat, you can be our friend.

We know reaching people who are far from God is extremely important in scripture, so we work very hard and spend good money on evangelism "projects". But once a new person starts coming, we quickly try to convert them, making sure they mind all the rules. We seem to have forgotten evangelism isn't something we do; evangelism is everything we are. The identity of Jesus is humility, self-sacrifice, and servitude. Jesus modeled all of these while He was on the planet and He continues the mission by sending us in the same manner He came. Jesus wasn't too good for sinners; one of the greatest insults the religious people could say of Him was He was a friend of sinners.

We have aspirations of reaching people who are far from God, but our budgets, time, attitudes, and relationships often reflect something entirely different. Think about it; ask yourself and your church some very hard questions. How much money did you/your church spend directly reaching out to people outside the Church last year? If you are a Christian, how many friends do you spend regular time with who are not churchgoers? Compare and contrast that to how much money you/your church spent on entertaining yourself or other Christians last year. Compare and contrast that with how much time you spent "fellowshipping" with people who are already going to Heaven for all eternity.

We have forgotten the mission of Jesus. The reason Jesus left Heaven and came to Earth is all about one thing: reaching people who are far from God. We are not supposed to be a safe exclusive club kneeling in the confines of our four little walls, desperately praying for God to instantly clean people up and bring them to us. The Church is supposed to be an all-inclusive mission to the world. We are supposed to be the hands and feet of Jesus reaching out and befriending all people.

What is the driving force behind exclusion?

The word *exclusive* means: high class, selective, excluding other things, elite, restricted, limited, and private. An extreme form of exclusion is segregation. The driving forces behind each of these terms are fear and selfishness. When the fear of the unknown (how they look, talk, act, and what they might do around or to our children) becomes our primary concern, our mission is completely derailed. When all we acre about is how we look and feel we are nothing more the consumers demanding our own way.

In reality we're not just afraid of outsiders, we're afraid of each other too. You have to be careful what you say around "so and so," because they will always blab it to everyone else. You have to be careful around "that person" because I heard he/she did "such and such." Our foyers and lobbies are filled with circles of people huddled around their trusted groups. Look what the Bible says about the spiritual condition of the person who lives in fear:

1st John 4:18 *"There is no fear in love. But perfect love drives out fear, because fear has to do with punishment. The one who fears is not made perfect in love." (NIV)*

The churches I attended in my formative Christian years got an A+ when it came to fear. These churches seemed to think evangelism was coercing people into attending church, praying the sinner's prayer, and behaving according to specific standards based on the sole fact they will go to Hell if they don't. So long as fear is constantly fed, it can keep people motivated for a very long time. Many people came to church based on fear, so perpetuating it only seemed natural.

Since the day they darkened the doors of the sanctuary, they were taught to dress, talk, behave, and pray according to very specific standards. Their adherence to the behavioral standards is what truly proved their devotion to Christ. This has kept many people "behaving" or at least pretending to behave for generations. But, this approach is no longer working. The children of the Boomer generation--the Buster's (my friends and I) and younger don't think in terms of fear or even black and white.

The younger generations are not scared. They are hurt, angry, disgusted, fed up, and burned out because the Church tries to manipulate them by "scaring the Hell out of them" with what they claim is the love of Jesus. Yes, I meant that to sound absurd. Many people left the Church because personal things were said or done directly to them. You may be reading this book because you feel it is about time someone said they were sorry. I want to say it again, "We are truly sorry." I also want you and the Church to realize the driving force behind all this dysfunction is FEAR and SELFISHNESS!

Fear robs intimacy and suffocates genuine love. The most effective thing fear does is produce more fear. Since so many of us were saved through fear, we not only reproduce it, we continuously live in it. During this series, I had a fifty-year-old man tell me he has just realized his entire relationship with God has been built on fear.

The greatest weakness of fear for the church is it drives us into defense mode. If you have ever seen a bear or rattlesnake backed into a corner, you understand exactly what I am talking about. The Church has felt threatened and scared of outsiders. When they feel backed into a corner, they react.

I regretfully admit the most painful experiences I have ever had came at the hand of other Christians. With even greater regret, I know others would say the very same thing, only with my face in mind. The Church is running scared, our relationships are superficial and tattered because fear has stolen true intimacy. This is why First John 4:18 says. *"There is no fear in love. But perfect love drives out fear, because fear has to do with punishment. The one who fears is not made perfect in love." (NIV)*

Jesus came to reconcile mankind in relationship to God. He begins this relationship long before we choose to receive Him as Leader and Lord. He loves and accepts us while we are completely unlovable. God loves you so much that He gave His Son for you. He is not a mean ogre itching to send people to Hell. If He was, He would simply get it over with. God loves all people and so should the Church.

Here is a passage of Scripture that is often used to motivate people with fear.

2 Peter 3:8-14 "Don't overlook the obvious here, friends. With God, one day is as good as a thousand years, a thousand years as a day. God isn't late with his promise as some measure lateness. He is restraining himself on account of you, holding back the End because he doesn't want anyone lost. He's giving everyone space and time to change. But when the Day of God's Judgment does come, it will be unannounced, like a thief. The sky will collapse with a thunderous bang, everything disintegrating in a huge conflagration, earth and all its works exposed to the scrutiny of Judgment. Since everything here today might well be gone tomorrow, do you see how essential it

is to live a holy life? Daily expect the Day of God, eager
for its arrival. The galaxies will burn up and the elements melt
down that day—but we'll hardly notice. We'll be looking the
other way, ready for the promised new heavens and the
promised new earth, all landscaped with righteousness. So, my
dear friends, since this is what you have to look forward to, do
your very best to be found living at your best, in purity and
peace." (MSG)

During the *hell, fire, and brimstone preaching* era, the latter half of this verse was stressed with great volume and fervor. Many people forgot the first half. The reason Jesus has not come back for over two thousand years is because God longs to have a personal relationship with all people. The reality of the final judgment of God and the earth being destroyed will happen. However, right now we are living in the time of God's grace. God loves the world so much that He gave His One and Only son, so that all people could be brought back into relationship with Him and not experience eternity separated from Him.

Many churches have changed their style of preaching, but their fear tactics and attitudes remain the same. There has been far too much attention placed on eminent judgment and far too little on the amazing patience and love of the Father. The Bible is clear that no one presently knows nor will anyone ever know how much longer it will be before Jesus comes back. (Matthew 24:36) In addition, Scripture couldn't be clearer on the fact that every day He waits is another day of His patient love for us.

I'm sure you have heard the Bible says the fear of the Lord is the beginning of wisdom. That is absolutely true; you can pick up any concordance, look up the word *fear*, and you will find dozens of verses exhorting us to fear the Lord. Why does God teach us this? Because the fear of the Lord is the only fear that frees us. To quote my favorite author (Erwin McManus): "When we fear God, we fear no one and nothing else." The fear of the Lord is the one fear that frees us from all other fears. Nothing is bigger or stronger than God and nothing can separate us from Him, not even death. Fearing Him is simply saying to Him, "I yield all that I am and all that I will ever be to your will and your ways". This fear liberates us, setting us free from all other fear. The fear of God is healthy.

Unfortunately the Church doesn't fear God. They fear people... People infecting their kids, people influencing members away from they're church, people leaving if they don't get what they want. The list of the fear of man could go on and on. It is hard to admit, but we are scared to death of people outside the Church and this fear has driven us into seclusion. The worst part about this fact is the rest of the world doesn't feel like we are afraid of them, they feel like we hate them, think we are better than them, and do everything we can to exclude them. We didn't maliciously intend for this to happen nor is this who we aspire to be, but fear causes us to do irrational things.

When we gave our lives to Jesus, our lives radically changed for the better. We now see life, God, and people through entirely different lenses than we did before we gave our lives to Christ. The new life we live in Christ took away all our guilt, shame, and self-destructive behaviors. Once we possess this new life our natural tendency is to protect it.

Proceed with Caution

Have you ever noticed how cautious you are when you have something to lose? When we're young and have no responsibilities, we live it up, risk big, and go for it. Why? We have nothing to lose. But as we age, we have more responsibilities, money, and valuable stuff. The more we obtain the more we have to lose, so we carefully protect all we have. When it comes to risking our children, family security, or provisions, what we need is wisdom not fear. Wisdom will keep us from making foolish and reckless decisions, but fear will drive a wedge between ourselves, God, people we love, and those who are outside the Church.

Many Christians are completely paralyzed when it comes to doing anything great for God. Many Christians, as well as churches, have dug deep trenches around their families only to see their teenagers defect, dig new foxholes, and become the enemy. Many Christians feel superior to the rest of the world and truly believe they are acting in holiness as they follow the overwhelming compulsion they feel to protect and defend their beliefs. Sadly, their fear has turned to anger, their anger to hatred, and they are left alone, unable to give love to anyone.

In an effort to stay close to Jesus, we avoid people who do things that tempt us or threaten our beliefs. If we have children, we proceed with even greater caution. The mere thought of drugs, alcohol, smoking, sex, babies outside of marriage, sexually transmitted diseases, kidnapping, human trafficking, tragic accidents, or anyone bringing harm to our kids is absolutely terrifying. Just writing those words make me want to grab my kids, hold them as close as I can, and never let them out of my sight. We have this built-in caution light flashing in the forefront of our minds saying, "Danger, Danger! Keep away! Proceed with great caution!" The more we have to lose the more cautious we become.

The product of our fear is exclusion. In our zeal, we have not only excluded outsiders. We have driven away the precious ones who faithfully attended week after week. Many kids who grew up in church want nothing to do with it. People are no longer looking to the Church for help. In fact, the Church isn't even a blip on the radar screen of society anymore. The Church has become so fearful that our seclusion has turned us into a strange subculture most people don't understand or want to be part of. What are we teaching? What are we perpetuating?

Church 101

The first thing I learned in church, and subsequently the first thing I taught people when I began in ministry, was what to avoid. The Bible says bad company corrupts good character. (1 Cor. 15:33 NIV) The Bible says not to be unequally yoked. (2 Cor. 6:14 KJV) Our church used these Scriptures to teach us to stay away from people who were not believers. Our friends had to be Christians because being friends with people who weren't Christians would influence us to sin. It literally felt like the Church thought sin was an infectious disease that would infect anyone who got within ten feet of a sinner. To be fair, they did want us to be friends so long as we invited them to church, but if they refused or didn't conform to our behaviors when they came, we were told to stay completely away from them.

Not only did they want our friends to be Christian, they wanted *all* our friends to be at *our* church. I later learned they were petrified of us leaving their church because we found a better church with an *outsider* friend down the street. Whatever the motivation was, friendships were a regular topic in Sunday school, church services, and youth group.

My parents bought into this teaching for a while, becoming increasingly more paranoid of all my "non-Christian" friends. One day, we gave a new kid at school a ride home from practice. I wanted to be able to hang out with him, so I went to the door to meet his parents when we dropped him off. As I got back in the car my mom was frantically waving her hand back and forth from her mouth saying, "He's a smoker, he's a smoker!" The very thought of her eighth grade son being friends with a smoker was enough to put her brain on full tilt. I didn't think he was a smoker and was feeling very defensive so I said, "So what, what if he is? I don't smoke, he needs friends, too!" When I said that, something very profound in the spiritual realm shook my mom's spirit. It was like the Holy Spirit was my wingman and my mom realized that what we were being taught at church might be a little off. She knew Jesus would befriend this kid. If Jesus would than so should we. We could be a positive influence in his life. We could invite him to youth group, take him camping with our family, and become a true friend. Hopefully one-day we would be able to share the forgiveness of Jesus with him and his family.

The other driving force behind church seclusion is selfishness. We put so much emphasis on potlucks, Bible studies, and fellowship we don't want to do anything else. Not that any of those things are wrong, but I have had way too many people tell me they don't want their church to change one single little bit. They love how small it is, they love that they know everyone and they feel safe there. One person recently said those exact words to me as we talked about her church and their building program. Before I knew it, I said, "its too bad God created so many people." She asked me to explain, so I continued, "Jesus said the Father's will is none be lost. God created almost seven billion people of which fifty-six thousand live within twenty driving minutes of her church. Remember, God created, loves, and brought every one of them to our city. He commands us to love, care for, serve, befriend, and show them the love of Jesus."

I asked her if she realized less than ten percent of the fifty-six thousand people in our community attend church, let alone have faith in Jesus. I had a real preach going so I concluded with, "God has commanded us to go to them." The next time I saw her, she apologized and confessed God had really convicted her heart and she was not only going to stay at her church, she was going to get involved with their missions and outreach team. Many church people don't notice new people when they come to their church because they are far too engrossed in "fellowshipping" with their friends. In many of our churches, new people don't feel like they are welcomed guests. I once heard Erwin McManus say, "Church fellowship is important, but for many churches it's like walking in on two people making out. It's intimate, but you don't feel like your supposed to be there."

Along with steering clear of worldly people, we were taught to absolutely stay clear of worldly behaviors. The Church seems to be constantly adding to he "worldly behaviors" list. We were not allowed to dress like the world, dance, listen to music unless it was written and sung by a Christian artist, watch movies or TV, play cards, gamble, and of course we should never drink, smoke, or chew, or go with girls who do.

Sadly, the Christian church has moved out of the world by building our exclusive little kingdoms. Many advocate kids should be homeschooled or go to Christian schools to keep them from being taught evolution, sex education, and all the social behaviors those schools advocate. We have our own gyms, we have Christian directories so we can avoid having outsiders work on our homes or fix our cars. We even have designer vacations labeled "Christian" so we don't have to be around outsiders during our time off. There are things we do in our world and most importantly, things we do not do. If you violate these standards or even appear to, your commitment is definitely in question and if you persist after being confronted, your salvation is too.

The general attitude is we are far better people than them. As I continue to study Scripture, I think it is abundantly clear that Jesus took a far different approach with His disciples. One great example is what Matthew did after he started following Christ:

Matthew 9:9-13 "As Jesus was walking along, he saw a man named Matthew sitting at his tax collector's booth. 'Follow me and be my disciple,' Jesus said to him. So Matthew got up and followed him. Later, Matthew invited Jesus and his disciples to his home as dinner guests, along with many tax collectors and other disreputable sinners. But when the Pharisees saw this, they asked his disciples, 'Why does your teacher eat with such scum?' When Jesus heard this, he said, 'Healthy people don't need a doctor—sick people do.' Then he added, 'Now go and learn the meaning of this Scripture: 'I want you to show mercy, not offer sacrifices.' For I have come to call not those who think they are righteous, but those who know they are sinners.'" (NLT)

Matthew threw a huge dinner party inviting his old tax collector buddies and his new disciple friends. Tax collectors were known liars, manipulators, and thieves. They were considered unclean and therefore excluded from entering the temple. Jesus not only went to the dinner, He brought the rest of the disciples with Him. They didn't get sloppy drunk, sleep with prostitutes, or hurt little children. They just had dinner. The religious leaders called the people at this dinner *scum*. "Why does Jesus eat with such scum?" (Matt. 9:11 NLT) This sounds dangerously close to the church I grew up in.

On my journey of faith I have encountered many self-righteous Christians who are unwilling to associate with non-Christians. To keep the excluded they gossip about them and slander everything they do. They not only slander them, they encourage others to slander them as well. Jesus was not teaching His disciples to act like sinners. Jesus taught them to be friends with sinners, because He trusted they were His true followers. "Greater is He that is in us than He that is in the world". (1 John 4:4 NKJ) True followers of Jesus lead others, not the other way around.

Kids are easily influenced, so I understand using discretion and wisdom in monitoring their friendships. With that said, I think we should realize we need to walk closely alongside, helping them learn how to navigate the real world. Not seclude, suffocate, or try to exclude them from it. Being a youth pastor for fifteen years, I saw many sheltered, controlled, and naive kids get swallowed up in college because they had no idea how to navigate what they were experiencing. I'm not just talking about secular college; I'm talking about Christian kids in Christian colleges.

I've seen many parents try to control their kids' every move, thinking they could demand what their kids believe, think, and do, only to find out later all they accomplished was complete alienation. Their kids have gone underground to find the answers they desperately needed. The problem is those answers came from the wrong people. Parents have been so fearful of outside influences they ban TV, music, movies, dancing, having friends of the opposite sex, and wearing anything that resembles the crowd. Many strong Christian families have pulled out of the public school systems because of fear. We have abandoned the very place that needs Christ's love, acceptance, and influence the most.

Every child is different and has different needs. There are very valid reasons to home school some kids or send some to private school, but fear should never be the driving factor. Christians point to the failures of the public school system, yet they refuse to be involved. Jesus prayed we would be in the world but not of the world. In fact, He said it would be impossible for us to leave the world, so He asked the Father to help us in it. (John 17:9-25 NLT)

Church 201

Faith 101 is all about excluding non-Christians/outsiders. It is an ongoing class we never actually graduate from so in conjunction with Faith 101 we simultaneously must master Faith 201. Faith 201 is how to discern whom to exclude on the inside. Faith 201 has to do with the church's desperate need to defend their doctrinal positions and denominational superiority. I grew up in a Pentecostal church, and I pastor one today. While growing up it was strenuously emphasized that Pentecostal's were far superior Christians, because we believe in "all" of Scripture because of the way we embraced "all" the spiritual gifts. There are other Pentecostal denominations, but we were taught that our denomination taught and expressed them in the correct manner. Staying true to our church and our denomination was extremely important. Once we got that straight, we could never forget that our church was the best in our denomination because... Well I am not sure why, except they were afraid we might leave and were very offended when anyone did. We rarely ever heard anything supportive of another church.

1ˢᵗ Corinthians 1:10-13 "I appeal to you, dear brothers and sisters, by the authority of our Lord Jesus Christ, to live in harmony with each other. Let there be no divisions in the church. Rather, be of one mind, united in thought and purpose. For some members of Chloe's household have told me about your quarrels, my dear brothers and sisters. Some of you are saying, 'I am a follower of Paul.' Others are saying, 'I follow Apollos,' or 'I follow Peter,' or 'I follow only Christ.' Has Christ been divided into factions? Was I, Paul, crucified for you? Were any of you baptized in the name of Paul? Of course not!" (NLT)

The apostle Paul was planting churches all over the known world. To him, you were either a follower of Christ or you weren't. There was only one Church of Jesus and it didn't matter if you attended the First Church of Corinth or Corinth Community Chapel. If you were a follower of Christ, you were supposed to protect unity in all the Christian churches. If you weren't a follower of Christ, you were one whom the Church was trying to befriend. Sadly, many churches in America are pitted against each other. The fastest way to know whether a pastor is truly following Scripture is to listen for him or her degrading/slandering other ministers or faith communities. I have had to ask the Lord to forgive me for this, too. Criticizing other churches is unscriptural and extremely sinful. All churches that teach Jesus as the only way to salvation are the same church. Our lineage extends all the way back to when Jesus began this movement with 12 guys near the Sea of Galilee.

Jesus said the world would know we are His disciples by our love for one another. (John 13:35 NIV) The opposite of this statement is true as well; the world will know we don't represent Jesus when we put each other down and fight over who has the most knowledge and best presentation. We can't afford to be divided about spiritual gifts, the expression of spiritual gifts, the way we do communion, enjoy different music styles, dress differently, or anything else. We should celebrate each other's strengths and cheer on our brothers and sisters who have different styles and philosophies of ministry. Our approach will not reach everyone, so we need to be different. This is the reason why God gave us so many different expressions of His body.

Remedial 101 and 201

Jesus taught us to be in the world but not of the world. The last prayer Jesus prayed before He was captured and taken to the cross is recorded in John 17. He prayed for you and me. Check this out:

John 17:15-18 "I'm not asking you to take them out of the world, but to keep them safe from the evil one. They do not belong to this world any more than I do. Make them holy by your truth; teach them your word, which is truth. Just as you sent me into the world, I am sending them into the world."
(NLT)

The reason Jesus doesn't want us to be taken out of the world is because He knows we can remain in it and still be made holy through the power and strength of the Holy Spirit in us. We need not try and prove to others we are better than they are. Holy is perfect and the only one who can accomplish holiness in us is God. We cannot earn the badge of holiness by attending the right church or doing all the right behaviors at all the right times. He makes us holy, and that is all we need to serve Him and see His kingdom advance through us.

Paul writes the church in Corinth because they had all kinds of immoral behaviors, distractions, and disunity happening in their church. While instructing them on how to deal with people who say they are Christians but continue in willful disobedience, he encourages them to continue associating with people who are far from God.

*1ˢᵗ Corinthians 5:9-13 "When I wrote to you before, I told you not to associate with people who indulge in sexual sin. **But I wasn't talking about unbelievers** who indulge in sexual sin, or are greedy, or cheat people, or worship idols. You would have to leave this world to avoid people like that. I meant that you are not to associate with anyone who claims to be a believer yet indulges in sexual sin, or is greedy, or worships idols, or is abusive, or is a drunkard, or cheats people. Don't even eat with such people. It isn't my responsibility to judge outsiders, but it certainly is your responsibility to judge those inside the church who are sinning. God will judge those on the outside; but as the Scriptures say, 'You must remove the evil person from among you.'" (NLT)* (Emphasis added)

Paul recognized the obvious: They weren't able to leave the world. Not being in relationships with people who are immoral is impossible. However, in American Christianity, we have the resources to totally seclude ourselves from the world. We have so much expendable income we don't have to leave the world; we can simply build our own. If we are going to be relevant in our culture, we will have to have relationships with them. People really don't care how much we know until they know how much we care. We must stop giving lip service to love. We must do what Jesus did. Go to them, befriend them, genuinely love them, and give our lives away for them. We need not fear being infected; greater is He that is in you than He that is in the world. (1 John 4:4 KJV) You can do all things through Christ who gives you strength. (Phil. 4:13 NIV) And so can your kids!

The love of Jesus is so compelling it can't help but burst out of us like living water... like springs of living water. The love and power of Jesus is strong enough to keep us close to Him. Especially as we love those who do not know Him yet.

The mandate of Christ is to go into all the world. (Matt. 28:19 NIV) Notice I did not say *commission*. We hear the word *commission* and think there is room to ignore it. The life of Jesus is all about reaching people who don't know Him. In fact, the whole Bible is about God's undying, unrelenting love for mankind. To be a Christ-follower and think we can avoid the world is missing the point of Scripture altogether.

We can't afford to compete with each other or argue about doctrine, methods of ministry, or style preferences. People who are outside the Church think we are a complete joke because we don't love each other even as much as their friends in the local taverns do. We have the most unifying conviction there is; yet we choose to focus on the minute details rather than the mission.

The Church is surrounded by friction. Praise God for that, because friction creates traction. The Church of Jesus can experience radical multiplication and people all over the world can find the love of Jesus and have true meaning and peace in their lives. It really is simpler than it seems; genuinely love people who are far from God and love each other. The love of Jesus is absolutely irresistible. Let's go public with it.

Questions:

1. Pray and ask God to open your heart to action steps He wants you to take.
2. What things in the world right now scare you?
3. What things in your community scare you?
4. Have you alienated yourself or your family from the world because of fear?
5. What changes do you need to make in your relationships with people outside the Church?
6. Have you ever put down or slandered another church?
7. Do you owe any past church leaders an apology for how you have talked to them or about them?
8. Do you owe any people from past or present churches an apology?
9. Do you owe friends, relatives, neighbors, or people in your community an apology for how you have talked to them, about them, or just plain excluded them from your life?
10. How can you exercise discernment, truly love people, and be involved while still remaining safe and or keeping your kids safe?
11. Do you think there is a link between exclusion, fear, and selfishness? How so?

Chapter 8:   Proud

Proverbs 16:18-19 "Pride goes before destruction, and haughtiness before a fall. Better to live humbly with the poor than to share plunder with the proud." (NLT)

Growing up, I played just about every sport available to me. All my confidence, and self-worth grew out of what I could do with my body. In the second grade, I saw the most amazing sport I had ever seen. I was sitting in our family room watching the *Wide World of Sports* on our twenty-five inch, console, color TV. You remember, "the thrill of victory and the agony of defeat." I sat absolutely mesmerized by a man running full-speed down a narrow runway with a giant jousting stick in his hands. As he sped down the runway, I looked for his opponent who would surely be coming in the opposite direction ready to take him out. As he ran, the view widened. Suddenly, the giant joust lowered, slid into a box on the ground, bowed into a giant sling, and flung the athlete over the crossbar eighteen feet in the air. It wasn't a jousting stick after all; it was called the "pole vault". In that moment, I fell in love with a new sport.

Every spring, I participated in track and field and couldn't wait until the eighth grade when I could start vaulting myself. Turns out, I was pretty good at it and in ninth grade I went undefeated winning the school district championship for all the junior highs in our area. Because of that great season, the track coaches from both high schools in our community came to talk to me. Promising to buy me a brand new pole specially fit for my size and weight. They "encouraged" me to go to their school. I thought I was pretty cool to say the least.

Going into high school, many thought I was sure to go undefeated, win state, and head off to the Olympics. My head was so big it was a wonder I was able to get on the bus and go to school! High school brought much deeper competition. There was always an upperclassman that seemed to get the best of me by at least three to six inches. However, placing second or third as an underclassman was extremely respectable.

As a senior year the spotlight was solely on me. The first meet of the season I won first place. Nothing could stop me now. The next week my girlfriend, who is now my wife, had a day off school so she spent the day going to school with me. The end of the day came and it was time for track practice. Tina was impressed when I parked my mustang on the field next to the pole vault pit, positioned the speaker box outside the car, instructed the track managers to get the pole vault mats out, and headed to the locker room to get ready. As I was going in, the assistant coach was coming out. He said, "Morgan, you're running today." He meant a long distance training run. This coach and I had a long history together, but to keep this story short, let's just say we didn't like each other. I said, "No, I'm not. My girlfriend is here and I am not going on a long distance run leaving her by herself." He said, "Yes, you are." I said, "No, I'm not!" He said, "You're either running or you're off the team." I said, "Fine, you need me more than I need you." Tina was absolutely shocked I would argue with my coach, let alone tell him off. She pled with me not to do it, but we got in my car, did a burn out on the field, and sped away.

For weeks, I was totally convinced I was absolutely right in my actions. Every time I rehearsed the conversation in my mind, I thought of even more hurtful things I wished I had said. Each time I relived the moment I got angrier than the last. In my mind my actions were feeling completely justified. The reason I kept going over this in my mind was because the Holy Spirit kept bringing it up. I had given my life to Christ and turns out God hates pride. In fact, I read in the Bible, "God opposes the proud"; He is literally against them. (Prov. 15:25 NLT) I wanted to be right with everything inside me, but deep down I knew I was dead wrong.

With the end of the season rapidly approaching I knew I had to apologize soon or risk losing the opportunity to make things right. Finally, one day after school I went to the locker room in search of the assistant coach. My heart was racing. I couldn't believe I was going to apologize to this tiny, little man whom I had a long history of despising. When our eyes met, I knew it was now or never. I had rehearsed this conversation in my head for days so I knew exactly what I was going to say. "Coach, I am very sorry for what I said to you and I am very sorry for quitting the team and being so arrogant." He accepted my apology and we both just stood there in awkward silence. He looked at me like I was going to plead to be back on the team, but I knew I didn't deserve it, and wasn't about to ask.

As I turned to walk away, he said, "Morgan, the Kingco Championship is next week. At the first meet of the season, you qualified to go. In fact, you are the number one seed. If you want to go, you can." Inside, I was so excited I could hardly stand it, but playing it cool, I gave a slight smile, a quick head nod, and said, "Yeah, I want to go. Thanks."

I hadn't practiced in almost two months. Prayer took on a whole new meaning that week. Before the meet began, I prayed with my mom. Before each attempt I visualized what I was suppose to do, prayed like crazy, and gave it all I had. I couldn't believe it, no practice in almost two months and I won first place! I was so thankful for God's help despite the fact I was such a prideful jerk. I honestly couldn't believe it.

I arrived Monday morning at school stoked over the win but humble because I Knew God helped me all the way. People were talking me up all day. My lifelong dream of going to state was back on the table. Having a great practice Monday coupled with friends bragging me up, by Tuesday my head swelled once again to the size of Texas! I sailed through the week, thinking I was the greatest thing since sliced bread. I was the number one seed going into districts and hadn't practiced in months.

The second seed was a guy I vaulted against for years. All through warm ups we talked smack and strutted our stuff like we were the greatest things since peanut butter met bread.

Jumping events always begin with the bar being set at a predetermined minimum height. Each athlete has the option of passing lower heights to avoid early fatigue. We of course, passed the lower heights knowing full well once we passed there was no going back. Looking on as the others attempted the lower heights we felt far superior to all.

By the time our turns came some of the competitors were already out of the competition. The number one seed always goes last so my fellow competitor went first. As he grabbed his pole he couldn't look more confident but... He missed! Looking at me and laughing, he walked passed and said, "No problem we got this." I stretched, did my pre-vault warm-up, visualized what I was supposed to do, said a small prayer, and attacked the pit with everything I had... missed. A few other competitors made it on their second chance and my biggest competitor was up again. Still fully confident, he set his marks, strutted down the runway, charged the pit, and... miss. This time as he walked by he said, "What the $%#&, the number one and number two seeds not making their opening height?" I thought to myself, "The number two not making it, the number one is about to take off." I set my mark, strutted down the runway, visualized the vault, said a bit larger prayer, and charged the pit, fully expecting to make it. Everything was going perfect until I reached the apex of the vault. My hip sagged as I turned to release the pole, barely clipping the bar... missed. A few others made it on their third attempt. By this time things were as serious as it gets. No more joking around, my opponent and I were extremely intent. His third and final attempt... misses. He didn't even look at me this time. Outwardly I kept my cool, but internally I was in full panic mode.

If I missed this vault, I would never go to state in my favorite and best event. This time I prayed all the way down the runway. Turned, closed my eyes, visualized the run, the plant, the hands gripping, my left elbow straight, the right knee driving into the air, the arch, extension, turn and release. I settled myself, took a deep breath and launched towards the pit. All my hopes and dreams of going to state, possibly vaulting in college, and the entire school knowing the outcome, riding on this one vault. The moment couldn't get any bigger for me……………………………….. I missed.

I never went to state in the pole vault. In fact, I never even came close to realizing my potential. I missed the whole season because of foolish pride. The sad thing was the competition wasn't that strong my senior year, but because of pride, neither was I. My ego was writing checks my body couldn't cash. (Hey Top gun was really popular that year.) God has a very effective remedy for pride. As you can see in my case, if we fail the first test, He will often give us a make up exam later. The bottom line is, God opposes the proud, but gives grace to the humble. If we choose pride, God will not stop us but pride often ends with the same result…failure and humiliation. The Bible calls this "a fall". I use the word humiliation because when a prideful person fails they can't help but feel humiliated because life is all about them. God loves us so much that He allows us to do life our way. We may find great measures of success along the way, but the higher we climb the further the fall. Pride always comes before a fall. (Prov. 16:18 NIV)

In this chapter, we will examine ways the Church has been

prideful. There are many. Pride is the breeding ground for all the areas we misrepresent Jesus. In our pride, we stick our noses in the air as we behave in complete hypocrisy. In our pride, we love the things of the world and strive for more and more money to obtain them. In our pride, we think we have the right to take the place of God and judge other peoples spiritual condition. In our pride, we have distorted sexuality and hidden in the shadows of our private sin. In our pride, we form political factions and battle for position in the Church. In our pride, we become enraged towards people who don't believe what we believe or act the way we want them to act. In our pride, we have formed a weird, sub-cultural bubble, keeping us isolated and protected from sinners.

Pride the most frightening of all attitudes, because it is so easy to spot in others, but almost impossible to detect in ourselves.

Americans pride themselves on being proud

We live in a world that celebrates, rewards, and encourages pride. People are attracted to self-made, self-confident, self-promoting professionals. We all want to win and if people don't believe in themselves, there's really no reason we should either. How many of us want to go to a surgeon who thinks they are "pretty good"? No one wants the investment firm managing their retirement portfolio advertising itself as "We're decent, we'll probably get you there"?

We love success; actually, it is the only acceptable option.

I'm not saying we shouldn't be good at what we do. In fact, I believe everything we do, should be done as unto the Lord. Whether I am writing a book, preaching a sermon, or mowing the church lawn, I should do it as if I am doing it for God. Doing great is not only a good thing it's a Godly thing. However, the better we do, the better we feel about ourselves. In many ways this is a God-given trait and there is nothing wrong with doing well and feeling good about it. Things become dangerous when the only way we sense any sort of satisfaction or joy is when we are the best. The more accolades we receive, the more tempted we are to believe our own press. Pride is a slippery slope.

As we experience success, acknowledgements go with it. This is where we must proceed with caution. Pride is a subtle lure that traps the heart and holds us captive in a prison of self-grandeur. Pride isolates us from others and destroys genuine love. Worse yet, pride isolates our spirit and keeps us from the heart of God. Self-importance needs no one or nothing. "Thank you very much God, but I can do it on my own."

Pride is something I have struggled with all my life. It's not that I think I am the greatest thing in the world. In fact, my greatest fear is that I am not enough. So, I tend to overcompensate with pride in an effort to convince myself, and others I have what it takes. My senior year pole-vaulting debacle was not my first rodeo with pride and I am ashamed to say it wasn't my last. God has a very effective remedy for pride.

Proverbs 16:18-19 "Pride goes before destruction, and haughtiness before a fall. Better to live humbly with the poor than to share plunder with the proud." (NLT)

Spiritual Pride

Pride doesn't just affect our natural life. Pride infects our spiritual lives. How is it possible for well meaning followers of Jesus to become full of pride?

When we gave our lives to Christ, the power of God came to live inside us through the Holy Spirit. This power is something we feel and know. When we gave our lives to Christ, we began to see the world differently and understand Scripture in a whole new way. As we apply Scripture we plant the very wisdom of God into the soil of our lives. As we plant God's wisdom, God's goodness grows in our lives.

Having the power of the Holy Spirit coupled with better results for our efforts feels incredibly powerful. Power gives us the sense of total control and before we know it we have fallen prey to the lure of pride. It's in our nature to desire success. We all long for success. Most of us pray for success, and work as hard as we can to obtain it. Even experiencing the slightest bit can become very tricky. Think about it. Dealing with failure is extremely challenging. Navigating difficult relationships requires incredible wisdom and patience. Coping with loss is heart wrenching and painful. And being hurt by people you trust can be devastating. Yet, in all the things we go through in life, the most difficult seas we will ever sail are the oceans of "success". Let's be real here, even the mud puddles of success can drown us if we are not careful.

God created us to work and produce. As we apply Scripture to every area of our lives, we often produce better results. The more we have, the more we are able to do. The more we do, the more we are able to produce.

Any success we achieve is because of his generous grace and love in our lives. In times of success, it is so easy to forget where all these great ideas come from. It's hard not to feel prideful when our efforts produce good results. The natural byproduct of success is the sense of accomplishment. In our accomplishments, we can find ourselves very quickly sliding down the slippery slope of pride.

Men and women are very different; therefore, they sense and experience pride in different ways. Tina had the hardest time understanding why I took such pride in my possessions until I bought a jacked-up, fire engine red Jeep CJ 7. It had a Chevy 350 motor, side pipes, 35 inch tires, tons of chrome, diamond plating, and racing bucket seats with 4 point harnesses; I mean… amazing! One hot sunny day, Tina drove the Jeep to the store with the top and doors off. As she pulled up to the stoplights, people complemented the Jeep. As she climbed down from the Jeep in the parking lot, more compliments. Everywhere she went she turned heads. Jeep plus hot chick, what do you expect right? Oops, there goes my pride again! When she got home, she said, "You can't help but feel cool driving this thing." Every time it was sunny she wanted my Jeep. She started to understand me in a whole different way that day.

Our spiritual and natural lives are woven together like a tight Persian rug. The natural by-product of following God is often success in one form or another. The Israelite nation wandered in the Sinai Desert for forty years. The Lord delivered them from slavery to the Egyptians. Once they were safely across the Red Sea, they began to complain and grumble against God. The older generation refused to trust God for His provision, so God made them wander for forty years until that unfaithful generation died. As God gets ready to take them into the Promised Land, He gives them a very clear warning about success. Check this out…

Deuteronomy 8:11-20 "But that is the time to be careful! Beware that in your plenty you do not forget the Lord your God and disobey his commands, regulations, and decrees that I am giving you today. For when you have become full and prosperous and have built fine homes to live in, and when your flocks and herds have become very large and your silver and gold have multiplied along with everything else, be careful! Do not become proud at that time and forget the Lord your God, who rescued you from slavery in the land of Egypt. Do not forget that he led you through the great and terrifying wilderness with its poisonous snakes and scorpions, where it was so hot and dry. He gave you water from the rock! He fed you with manna in the wilderness, a food unknown to your ancestors. He did this to humble you and test you for your own

good. He did all this so you would never say to yourself, 'I
have achieved this wealth with my own strength and energy.'
Remember the Lord your God. He is the one who gives you
power to be successful, in order to fulfill the covenant he
confirmed to your ancestors with an oath. But I assure you of
this: If you ever forget the Lord your God and follow other
gods, worshiping and bowing down to them, you will certainly
be destroyed. Just as the Lord has destroyed other nations in
your path, you also will be destroyed if you refuse to obey the
Lord your God." (NLT)

They honored God with their faithful obedience. As they followed God's decrees for everyday life, they experienced the benefits of following Him… His word works… We reap what we sow or another way to put it is, we get what we plant. As Christ-followers, we apply scriptural principles to our lives. The by-product of following God is doing better in all areas of life: business, love, friendships, and everything in between. The Bible works! As we experience success, it's very hard not to take credit for what we have accomplished through His wisdom. As the Lord warned the Israelites, when things were going good, it is easy to forget who rescued us from a life of sin and gave us the abilities and talents we have to earn a living. If you really think about it, the very breath we breathe is a gift from God. It is so easy to get caught up in success and feel like we made it all on our own.

Pride in What We Don't Do

Christian pride is probably greater perpetuated by what we abstain from. Often times following Godly principles requires us to deny worldly pleasures. In fact, Jesus said in Luke 9:23, "If anyone would come after me he must deny himself." We are well aware sin can bring temporary pleasure and excitement. At the same time, we know God asks us to stay away from sin because sin brings pain to ourselves, and those around us.

Because we choose to deny these things, we feel proud of the sacrifices we make for God. One of the easiest ways to detect pride is when we make sure people know about all the things we give up.

Because we believe these choices would be better for all mankind, we "expect" others to do the same. For example, when we honor God with our sexuality, marriages are stronger, families are stronger, and people aren't physically, emotionally, or mentally hurt by sexual deviancy. Because others sexuality management upsets us and goes against scripture, we feel we have the right to force others to do what we think is right.

Because we abstain from things God asks us to abstain from, we feel superior for what we don't do. At the same time we look down on others who do.

This pride is not only flaunted at those outside the Church. It might be worse towards those inside. Some Christians become so proud they appoint themselves the morality police. They feel so confident they actually think they have the right to enforce their convictions on everyone else. They attempt this control through manipulation, threats, and social blackballing. This is a significant reason so many people have left the Church and are so adamant about never returning.

Some Christians have the audacity to tell people how they must think, behave, and talk. Some go as far as telling people how to dress, walk, and even how to vote. In our self-righteous pride, we think we have the right to enforce our personal convictions on everyone in the world. Pride causes us to forget God is in charge and He has chosen to give all people free will.

God lets every person reap the benefits of good choices and suffer the consequences for the bad. God allows every person the right to choose what he or she will, or will not do. It is the epitome of pride to assert ourselves above God. When we think we have the right to take away others' free will, we are doing something even God doesn't do.

I wish I could say we stop there but it is far worse. Our pride has risen to such a level we judge people's spiritual condition. When others choose not to follow scripture or struggle with sin they wish they could overcome, we often threaten them with eternal damnation. What a scary thing; human pride thinking so highly of itself that it exalts itself above the King of Kings and the Lord of Lord's and makes a judgment that is never theirs to make.

Pride in What We Know

God's Word given to mankind is an extremely lavish gift. Among many things, the Bible is the revelation of God and the guide for life. The reason we know whom God is and what he does is because of His Word and the presence of the Holy Spirit in our lives. The reason we are able to overcome sin is because of the guidance of His Word and power of the Holy Spirit living inside us. The knowledge of the Heavenly Father through His Word has accomplished in us exactly what Jesus said He came to do in *John 10:10, "The thief's purpose is to steal and kill and destroy. My purpose is to give them a rich and satisfying life." (NLT)* The knowledge and application of Scripture is what has made our lives good.

The greatest temptation with knowledge is power. As Christ-followers, we have taken personal pride in the knowledge God afforded us. After the apostle Paul started the church in Corinth, he wrote them two letters. In his first letter, he says this about knowledge:

1st Corinthians 8:1-3 "Now regarding your question about food that has been offered to idols. Yes, we know that 'we all have knowledge' about this issue. But while knowledge makes us feel important, it is love that strengthens the church. Anyone who claims to know all the answers doesn't really know very much. But the person who loves God is the one whom God recognizes." (NLT)

Knowledge makes us feel important, but love strengthens the Church. Other translations say, "Knowledge puffs up". It makes us feel proud! Doesn't it drive you nuts to be around the Christian who thinks they know everything? They quote Bible verses for everything and aren't afraid to arrogantly spout them off everywhere they go. The Bible says the person who is always throwing verses in your face, they don't know very much at all.

I need to be clear about this. The Bible is not saying Christians shouldn't use their brains or obtain knowledge. In fact, *Proverbs 8:10 says, "Choose my instruction instead of silver, knowledge rather than choice gold."(NIV) Proverbs 10:14, "The wise store up knowledge, but the mouth of a fool invites ruin."(NIV)*

There are many passages of Scripture encouraging life long learning and constant growth. Gaining knowledge is one of the best investments you can make in yourself. However, we run the same risk with knowledge as we do with success. Knowledge gives us an edge, but that edge can often make us feel superior to others. Superiority exercises itself through pride.

Here's how it can look to an outsider; as we build relationships with people outside the Church, they share the stories of their lives with us. For instance, a friend confides in us, "My spouse doesn't trust anything I say, he/she is always mad at me." After more dialogue, we discover a pattern of half-truths and shady behavior. As our friend feels more comfortable and safe with us, they confess infidelity that happened in the past. We listen, try very hard to be empathetic, and give what we feel is solid and grace-filled advice. We've even helped them out with some of their immediate needs, but nothing seems to be changing. This goes on and on and on with no end in sight. To us, the answer seems obvious, but this friend hasn't quite figured it out yet. They continue complaining until finally we can't take any more, so we give them a dose of reality. We say something flippant and rude like, "If you don't like how it feels when you slam your head against the wall, stop slamming your head against the wall! Stop being so stupid!" We don't actually use these exact words, but to them that's what it sounds like.

Our tone and body language scream, "You're an idiot! You don't have a clue!" Our complete lack of grace and patience communicates prideful superiority. To us, the answers seem simple because God gives such clear guidance in His Word. In fact, many times it feels like people should be able to figure out a lot of their issues just using common sense and basic morals. But for whatever reason this person just doesn't see it. Because of our prideful outburst, the friendship either ends or becomes so fractured we stop seeing the person all together. In our pride, we blame them, declaring they just don't want the truth.

This is why many people, including Christians, don't feel safe talking to Christians about real life issues. Christians are supposed to represent the love, compassion, and mercy of Christ. But when given the opportunity to do so, our pride often spews out Christian clichés, superior attitudes, and harsh judgments. We come across arrogant because we think we have everything figured out. Deep down we might really care and truly want to help, but our pride alienates and drives people away. Pride leads us deeper into the lonely pit of self-grandeur.

People don't care how much you know until they know how

much you care

Having the grace, mercy, and forgiveness of Jesus should make it very easy to be patient and kind to all people no matter what they say or do. But for some reason, it is very hard to show these qualities of Christ to people who continually disobey God. It is even harder to show grace, mercy, and love towards people who vehemently oppose our faith, ridicule our ethics, and encourage others to do the same. With that said, we must remember Jesus continues to extend the hand of forgiveness to all people... "Even the people who nailed Him to the cross". If anyone has the right to judge or enforce rules and regulations it's Jesus. But He never did.

Have you ever done the right thing the wrong way? The Christian Church may be right about many things, but our attitude comes across so arrogantly, people don't care. People are not feeling the love of Christ because it is impossible to experience love through pride. You can be right as rain, but if you communicate it the wrong way, it doesn't make a difference.

The old saying: people don't care how much you know until they know how much you care. Is absolutely true. God has called us to genuinely love and accept people just the way they are. We must extend them the same gifts of free will, love, and compassion God gives us. We must allow them to make their free choices and suffer the consequences or reap the rewards. One of the most difficult things about knowing the Word of God is accepting the fact we can't control others; even when their choices directly affect us, our children, the country, and sometimes the entire world. The problem with humanity is we hate not being in control.

All we need is love

So, where do we go from here? The great philosopher Paul McCartney said it well: "All we need is love." One of the greatest debates of our time is: what is love and how should it be expressed? We have terms like "tough love", "free love", "easy love", "true love", etc. etc. As I study the life of Christ, one thing seems to always ring true: love flows from a heart of humility. In the shadow of the cross love would be defined by humility. Some Christians think sharing their faith is all about defending the Word of God and attacking those who disobey it.

It sickens me to see people use the name of Christ and quote Scripture while they pick fights against organizations or causes that violate the morality of God's Word. Whenever we take a defensive posture, we automatically lose; as if we are strong enough to defend God.

Think about how silly this would look. We are walking the streets of our town in the dark of the night. God is standing behind us, in all His immensity, power, and strength. And this puny little kid (me) standing in front of Him says, "If you want Him, you will have to go through me!" God does not need our defense. We are incapable of defending Him. Pretending we can is nothing but arrogance. God does not need me to enforce anything. This is why He gave us the job of reconciliation not superior court judge.

The Bible says it is the kindness of God that leads us to repentance. Our example is Jesus; the one they called a friend of sinners. Those who live for debates and/or pick fights with those who do not believe in God are full of pride. It is pride that makes us feel we have the right to defend God and demand our way. Pride makes us believe being right is all that matters. As Paul said, "Knowledge makes us feel important, but love builds up the church."

You might wonder if I am advocating we never share the truth. Nothing could be further from my heart. Scripture teaches us to tell the truth in love. As distasteful as arrogance is, it is equally disturbing to see Christians not share at all.

- Many Christians are afraid of being associated with the antagonistic radicals.
- Many Christians are afraid of being attacked by the other side.
- Many Christians feel unprepared and have no idea what to say or how to say it. So they say nothing at all.
- Many Christians are terrified of people not liking them.

If I had a nickel for every time a Christian said, "We just need to live it", I would be a very wealthy pastor. For some reason Christians have become convinced we can just be around others and the holiness of God will be so strong in our presence that people will feel compelled to give their lives to Christ. How arrogant is this? Jesus was the holiest person to ever walk the planet and this was clearly not His approach. We must share our faith. I love what the well-known atheist, magician Penn said, "How much do you have to hate someone if you truly believe they are going to Hell and you know how to save them, yet you choose to do nothing?" That is exactly what it would be, hate. What we need is love. We need to love all people and genuinely care about them, not control them.

The only people Jesus was defensive or rude to were the religious people who flaunted their successful positions. Jesus was rude to the arrogant religious leaders, but was kind, compassionate, truthful, sacrificial, and forgiving to sinners. He not only lived a holy life, He shared His forgiveness, love, and compassion to people whom Christians today would consider very far from God.

Genuine love is shown when we live an authentic Christ-like life coupled with sharing the Good News of His salvation and abundant life with grace, humility, and gentleness. Unfortunately, our pride has gotten the best of us. The message of God's amazing love, compassion, mercy, and grace for all mankind is to be lived out and spoken of by all His followers. Christians should be taking the high ground when they are insulted, challenged, or attacked. We must apply Scripture to ourselves and stop forcing it on others.

Romans 12:17-21 "Do not repay anyone evil for evil. Be careful to do what is right in the eyes of everyone. If it is possible, as far as it depends on you, live at peace with everyone. Do not take revenge, my dear friends, but leave room for God's wrath, for it is written: 'It is mine to avenge; I will repay,' says the Lord. On the contrary: 'If your enemy is hungry, feed him; if he is thirsty, give him something to drink. In doing this, you will heap burning coals on his head.' Do not be overcome by evil, but overcome evil with good." (NIV)

God wants us to overcome evil the same way Jesus did: with LOVE. There is no greater love than this – than to lay down your life for your friends. Although some followers of Christ have become actual martyrs and more will probably follow, most of us reading this book don't actually have to literally give our lives. We are called to be living sacrifices. This means we lay down our rights and serve other's interests rather than demand our own way. Imagine the impact we could have if we served all people. Imagine how the love of Christ would spread if we humbled ourselves like Christ humbled Himself.

Humility is not thinking less of yourself. Humility is thinking of yourself less.

The fruit of the spirit is love, joy, peace, patience, kindness, goodness, gentleness, faithfulness, and self-control. This fruit is obtained by humbling ourselves, and giving all we are and all we have to Jesus. Let's not be tricked into thinking we are special because of the amazing things God has done in our lives. Let's not be tricked into thinking we are better than others because of the changes God has made in us. Let's not allow our heads to swell and miss out on the most important event of all time.

I never went to state in the pole vault because of my foolish pride. I don't want to miss the season of eternity because of pride. We don't want ourselves or anyone else to miss the ultimate victory of Heaven because of pride.

Prayer

- Ask God to reveal any pride you may have.
- Confess the pride He brings up and ask Him to help you be a humble servant.

Questions:

1. What are the three things you are most proud of in your life?
2. Have you ever had a pride wake-up call? What was it?
3. Do you notice any spiritual pride in your life?
4. On a scale of one to ten, one being like Jesus and ten being like me in the pole vault, how would people who are not Christ-followers rate your level of pride?
5. Is there anyone you need to apologize to for being proud? When are you going to do it?

We're Sorry

Conclusion

Final Words to Those Inside the Church

If you are a Christian, I want to thank you for reading this book all the way through. I realize these chapters can be extremely offensive. In fact, as I preached through this series, I was constantly challenged to examine many of the things I have said and done as they pertain to each chapter. I have had multiple failures in almost every area.

In second Corinthians, the apostle Paul wrote to the church in Corinth. Corinth was a church that had all kinds of dysfunction and sin. In chapter five of his second letter, he reminds them that they are the people who represent Jesus. When the people of their community see them, they see who Jesus is.

Since the time Jesus said goodbye to His disciples, we have been left with the ministry of reconciling the world to God. There have been countless disciples of Jesus over the past two thousand years since Christ and each of us has carried the torch in our time. In North America today, those outside the Church do not hold the Christian Church in high regard. My greatest prayer is for us to stay true to the calling we have received from our Lord. While at the same time not compromising our commitment, nor watering down the Word of God just so we can fit in.

I think we can tell the truth in love. I think we can love all people and accept them as fellow human beings who are created and loved by God. I think we can be genuine friends with people who do not want anything to do with God. I believe with all my heart, as we love them, they will see the love of God through us. *They don't have to convert to Christianity to be our friends, but we have to be their friends if we are going to stay true to Christianity.*

There is a tremendous amount of friction between those inside and those outside the Church. The heat is coming from both sides, but in my opinion, I think we are most to blame. We are supposed to love, help, and care for all of mankind. In many ways, we have done just the opposite. As I said earlier, "Where there is friction there is traction." If we will humble ourselves, apologize, and repent by changing our attitudes, words, body language, voice tones, and looks of disgust, we have a greater chance at truly building a bridge of friendship with people who do not believe what we believe.

If we choose to love people, we will become a very positive influence for Christ. Jesus did not win every person in His day, but He did love and befriend all people who were outside the Church. We must do the same.

I believe that deep in the heart of most Christians is a deep love for God as well as a deep love and concern for all mankind. We live in one of the greatest times in history when it comes to sharing the love of Christ on a global scale. This is something I know we can get better at and my prayer is we all sincerely give ourselves to the process.

Final Words to Those Whom Don't Attend Church

If you are a person who is outside the Church, been hurt by the Church, or someone who flat-out does not believe in God or the Bible, I want to sincerely apologize for the ways we in the Church, have mistreated you. Because I am a Christ-follower, I believe you are a person who is created by God and for that reason, you are not only a person who deserves respect, you also deserve genuine friendship and love. I have not always treated all people with love and respect. I am very sorry for what I have said and done. I am also sorry for what many others, who claim my same beliefs, have said and done in the name of Christ as well.

Thank you so much for reading my book. I hope and pray that we not only peaceably co-exist in this world; I pray we can be genuine friends and respect each other as fellow human beings. As Christians, we have not always followed and obeyed the words of Scripture. We have failed you and the Heavenly Father. I realize it would be presumptuous of me to apologize for all Christians, but I know I can on behalf of our church and many others who have cheered us on in this process. We're sorry. Please forgive us.

I hope and pray this book impacts our culture in such a way that we all become willing to come back to the table of conversation, find common ground as fellow human beings, and engage in friendly conversations about the meaning and purpose of life.

Made in the USA
Charleston, SC
05 January 2014